Pedagogy of the Earth

About the editors

Dr. Carlos Hernandez, President, New Jersey City University, is one of the leading international thinkers and educationists in the world. Dr. Hernandez has been a Governor's appointee, New Jersey State Education Department, since 1990. Besides receiving several awards, prizes and citations, he has received the prestigious Priyadarshini Award in India for 'Education and Development' in 1994. He delivered a major address on environmental education at the Earth Summit of the U.N. in Rio and has participated in several international conferences. He is an eminent writer and speaker on education and sustainable development worldwide.

Dr. Rashmi Mayur is a well-known expert in environment and international development. He is an ecologist, globalist and a futurist. He has been an Advisor to several agencies of the United Nations and governments in the developing world on the issues of environment, education and sustainable development.

Dr. Mayur, a professor at New Jersey City University, has taught and lectured extensively in several universities around the world including Harvard, MIT, University of Bombay, Tokyo Institute of Technology, University of Rio, Moscow University and many other institutes.

He has been a featured speaker at all the recent United Nations conferences. He was an inaugural speaker at the Earth Summit NGO Forum. His writings are published worldwide. He has received several international awards.

About the book

"If knowledge is power & power can change the world, then <u>*Pedagogy of the Earth*</u> *serves the most significant purpose of educating common people about the environment. Very few books have the power of the* <u>*Pedagogy.*</u>*"*

—Noel Brown
Ex-Director, UNEP, USA

"This is a book of voices of the earth. Those who care for our future, must listen to these voices by reading it."

— Dorival Correira Bruni
President, BIOSFERA, Brazil.

"This book should be a required reading for everyone. Any one reading this book, will become a true crusader of the Earth."

—Edward Cornish
President, World Future Society, USA.

" Hernandez & Mayur have taken up the challenge of saving the earth by educating people about environment & ecology. Their task is ominous. But their optimism scintillates through the pages of this prophetic book. Every one who cares for our environment must read it."

— Snehalata Deshmukh
Vice-Chancellor, University of Bombay, India

"We need to read two types of books : one, a book of Nature, which we read by living with her and becoming one with her. The other a book about Nature, which takes us to her fold. Dr. Hernandez and Dr. Mayur have prepared a book of a sacred message of living with the earth before she dies because of our wanton lifestyle."

— Hildur Jackson, Vice President
Gaia Trust, Denmark

"This is a rare book of education—for those devoted to making the world a better place to live".

— Patrick Portway,
Executive Director, Global Distance Learning Association, USA

Other books by the Editors :

Earth, Man and Future

Learning For the New Millenium

Millenium

Pedagogy of the Earth

Education for A Sustainable Future

Edited and Written
by
Carlos Hernandez, Ph.D
and
Rashmi Mayur, Ph.D

Published by
International Institute for Sustainable Future,
and
Bharatiya Vidya Bhavan
Mumbai, India.

vi

Published by the International Institute for Sustainable Future
and the Bhartiya Vidya Bhavan.

Ó **International Institute for Sustainable Future, 1999.**
Copyright acknowledgements on page 243

First Published April 1999

International Institute for Sustainable Future
73A, Mittal Tower,
Nariman Point,
Mumbai - 400 021.
India.
Tel: +91-22 204 5758
Fax: +91-22 287 1250
E-mail: iisfb@giasbm01.vsnl.net.in

ISBN No. 81–87404–00–01

Printed at
Shree Rajmudra
Prabhadevi, Mumbai 400 025

Contents

List of boxes

Acknowledgements

This book originated with two remarkable human beings — Lillan (wife of Carlos) and Kumudini (Rashmi's sister). We have had many discussions with them on the environment, global development and human future which led to the preparation of plans for writing this book with the hope that one day information and knowledge in it will lead to sustainable development worldwide. We are profoundly grateful to them for their inspiration. We must, however, recognize Lily specially since she has been the pillar and spirit behind the project of writing books on environment and sustainable future.

We must express our personal gratitude to the Board of Trustees of the New Jersey City University, particularly Mr. John Moore, Chairman; Dr. William Symes and Girish K. Chitalia, Co-Chairmen of the Global Futures Network, an affiliate to the United Nations and Prof. Jayant Shah for supporting the project of writing this and other books. We could not have carried on this project which demands extensive research, travels, and the concentration without their cooperation.

Among the many members of the administrative staff of the New Jersey City State University, two names deserve special mention: Mr. John Nevin, Vice President, a true global and progressive thinker and Ms. Maria Cobarrubias, Assistant to the President, whose dedication, commitment, energy and leadership are supreme.

Many leading ecologists, educators and thinkers have contributed extensively in preparing the book. They are:

Dr. Lester Brown, The WorldWatch Institute; Mr. Edward Cornish, President, World Future Society; Dr. & Mrs. Ross and Hildur Jackson, Gaia Trust; Dr. Darshan Johal, Director, United Nations, Center for Human Settlements; Dr. Frederico Mayor Director General, UNESCO; Ms. Carmen Melendrez, State of the World Forum; Mr. Patrick Portway, Executive Director, Global Distance Learning Association; Dr. Maurice Strong, the Secretary General, the Earth Summit, 1992; Dr. Klaus Topfer, Executive Director, UNEP, and Mr. Sashi Tharoor, Special Advisor, Secretary General, United Nations. We are indebted to them for there guidance.

Among many experts we consulted regularly during the long period of research and writing, we would like to mention at least some of them since it is impossible to list everyone. We are greatful to them. They are:

Mr. Adnan Amin, Director, UNEP, North America, Dr. Noel Brown, Ex-Director, UNEP, North America, Ms. Selma Brackman, President, War & Peace Foundation, Mr. P.P.Chabbria, Chairman, Finolex Cables India Ltd., Mr. Charles Brewer, Chairman, Learnsat Corp. Dr. Snehlata Deshmukh, Vice-Chancellor, Mumbai University, Mr. Bennett Daviss, eminent futurist and writer, Mr. Lucien Deschamps, Director, Energy Dept. France, Dr. Luis Gomez Echeverri, UNDP, Mr. Darryl Greer, Dr. Gary Herbertson, President, Earth Day International, Mr. Kamelendra Kanwar, Dr. Bir Maker, Mr. Ratanlal Parasrampuria, Mr. Stanley Rustin, Dr. Arnold Spreer, Dr. Shantilal Somaiya, Mr. R. V. Shahi, Mr.Virendra M. Trehan, Mr. James Walls.

We are indebted to Ms. Roshni Udyavar, who worked extensively assisting us with research and writing the book. Also, Dr. K. B. Jacob helped in research and screening the literature. We are fortunate to have had expert editors for extensive editing and putting the final manuscript in publishable order: Ms. Carol Andrade, Mr. Avinash Kolhe and Mr. Rajendar Menen. Finally, we must thank the staff of the Global Futures Network for computerization and the production of the book: Ashok Kumar, V. S. Nair and A. S. Saravanan.

Lastly, we cannot forget our appreciation to the innumerable people whom we encountered during more than two years of research and travels. Their contribution is equally significant.

Finally, our real inspiration and knowledge came from our beautiful Earth — monkeys, elephants, peacocks, parrots, lotuses, deers, mountains, oceans and the sacred trees of the Amazon, Brazil and the Silent Valley, India. We express our abiding reverence for them for teaching us the eternal values of life and its purpose.

Introduction

Down below lies a solitary continent of Australia with inauspicious climates and inhospitable environment. During the last 60,000 years, it has been inhabited by some of the most pre-technological people known as Aborigines. A disaster occurred, so an Aborigines myth tells us,10,000 years ago. Massive floods inundated the land and much of the life disappeared when famine followed, but some humans, birds and animals survived on the mountains.

When the disaster was over, the wise men and women began channeling themselves to *Baiame*, the great spirit about whom they had heard from their ancestors. They asked *Baiame* to ensure the survival of their race. *Baiame* listened to them with sympathy and asked his friends *Nungeena* (Mother Nature), *Punhel* (the architect of the Universe) and *Yhi* (Sun goddess) to assist the desperate humans to survive and continue their race. They all agreed to resolve the crisis of the Earth by instructing all men and women how to respect creation and live in accordance with the laws of *Nungeena*. Soon they found that the earth became a paradise — lush vegetation, abundant fruits, berries and fish and good life for everyone. They lived in happiness for many eons to come.

This myth tells the truth about our fundamental relationship with the earth. The Aborigines knew it. We have lost it. Our ignorance, or better, our arrogance, has put the earth under seige and us in jeopardy. Do we know who we are in relation to the larger scheme of things and what we are doing? Do we realize that our existence on this unique planet is a rare opportunity? Do we know where our journey is taking us to? Despite all our claims to enormous knowledge, mysteries of life and earth abound. We are yet to acquire real knowledge of us and *Gaia*— Mother Earth.

The Aborigines knew because their experiences through the ages taught them to deal with their much simpler world. Laotse, the wise man of China, once said, "You can learn by seeing inside" — by understanding the laws of Nature, and when we understand them, we must live by them. In the end, actions change the world. Paulo Freire, a Brazilian educator, emphasized that learning means becoming critically aware of our pathological reality and then bringing the positive changes. In short, we must learn in order to transform.

Those of us, who understand the state of Earth in its myriad complexities and crises, feel deep in our hearts that there is something amiss about life and the world we live in. We are saddened by its destruction. Wise American Indians used to ask: Do we know what will happen to our seventh generation? More profound question for us is: will there be a seventh generation? Many environmentalists agree with the warning of the Union of Concerned Scientists: If we continue on the present doomsday path, earth will be liquidated sometime in the next millennium. The warning is based on the examination of the biological, chemical, and physical systems of the Earth, which have remained quite stable for more than four eons, when life originated. Humans are the first species during all these geological times to threaten the stability of the earth.

The Earth summit of the UN in 1992, a historical event, was the first effort of humanity to chart a path to mend the despoliation wrecked by our species, mostly during the last 300 years of technological revolution. But, how many people in the world know or have read its blueprint — the Agenda 21— a global plan of action to bring sustainability? And how many governments, which signed the agreement, have implemented the Agenda? Meantime, as we emphasized earlier, many thinkers all over the world recognize that our Earth is dying, life is being threatened, humans in large part of the world are becoming pathological or are suffering in miseries.

This is an age of science and technology. For the first time in human history, we have built a technological civilization, which pervades through every continent. The basic premise of this civilization is to bring development at any cost. It is only during the last five decades that the erroneous nature of the assumption has been understood and questioned. Now we understand the grim consequences of the runaway technologies evident universally. Add to that, the problem of the reckless multiplication of our numbers. We are already near 6 billion people and in 1999, 78 million more will be added and the growth will continue practically through the next century. Meantime, our consumption continues to expand exponentially. The ill consequences of all these malignant developments has brought us to the present brink of demise.

Too long, we have remained oblivious to these crises; although our knowledge concerning many of these problems have continued to expand. We have undertaken the task of writing this book with a hope that knowledge and its application will change the path of despoliation of our environment and ecology. Great Greek thinker, Seneca said long ago, "I am glad to learn". Learning is what we humans do. In fact, we are the only learning creatures on the planet, and our survival depends on it.

For us the moot question is not about learning but what we should learn and know and what we do with our knowledge. Many fundamental truths about our relationship with nature have been known to us since time immemorial. People in almost all pre-technological societies always lived in harmony with nature.

Most of these societies were based on the values of preservation of ecology. It is only recently that our learning about ecology and our relationship with the earth have been neglected and ignored. Our values have been distorted. We are told that the main objective of knowledge is to increase the material wealth for progress. This book is a challenge to the distorted purposes underlying our civilization. Our search is to know the plight in which we are today and where we are going if we continue on the distorted path we have been pursuing blindly.

The Pedagogy of the Earth is a book of knowledge, of our understanding of the earth, of us as human beings and finally of our plans to create a world based on ecological values— a world of harmony and sustainability, a world which would be good for our children and their children until the evolution takes us to the next stage. We are not thinking about building a technological utopia. Our task is more modest. We want to correct the aberrations, which have allowed us to build a celluloid world of deceptions. If pursued ignominiously, it is the sure path to extinction.

Therefore, recognising that all our knowledge ultimately has a normative purpose, we would like the people everywhere to build a new society based on intrinsic values of life such as simplicity, harmony, cooperation, conservation, equity, justice and love. *The Pedagogy of the Earth* expresses the voices of nature; it narrates ideas and philosophies; it articulates the voices of the voiceless in the form of poetry, myths and folk tales. It has stories from everywhere—not just from the West. In short, the book gives a kaleidoscopic panorama of the rich material, which, we hope, will bring a global transformation—a transformation, which will free us from the technological prison and bring hope by integrating humans with the grand design of the magnificent Nature. As an Aborigines dreamtime story admonishes, "Let us go back home".

Are we ready for such a profound transformation? Is it possible for our knowledge to bring hope? Do we want future? We do not know, but we can all try if we care for our children. If we succeed, we shall have a good earth to enjoy. We believe that the light of knowledge will bring a hope of a new morning so that the children will have tomorrow—to dance to the music of the rising Sun.

Carlos Hernandez, Ph.D.
Rashmi Mayur, Ph.D.

" I danced in the morning
when the world was begun
and I danced in the moon
and the stars and the sun
and I came down from heaven
and I danced on the earth .... "

-- Sydney Carter.

Why Earth Education !

" Most educators would continue to lecture on navigation while the ship is going down. "

— James H. Boren

FLOWERS OF DREAM

It was all dark
When I arrived
in the morning
of life.
Soon I realized that
I exist.
It was dawn,
but still dark.

Then the world
Was revealed to me.
The sun had already
risen.
I was blinded
as if the night had
returned.
Suddenly I knew
and there was
lightening
at the end of the horizon.

I was enlightened.
I learnt
That it was
all dark
beyond the sun.
Then I learnt
that in the vast
ocean of knowledge,
I knew infinitesimal-
I knew nothing.
I was only
Searching.

It thundered in the
cosmos.
Then it was light
everywhere.
The sun was no more.
Ah! Flowers bloomed
in full glory.
The stars danced
in ecstasy.
And life became
a creative dream.

— Rashmi Mayur

Education for Sustainable Development

Carlos Hernandez and John Nevin

The ultimate value of life depends upon awareness and the power of contemplation rather than upon mere survival.

— Aristotle

Since the early 1960s, Third World development has been a golden promise which has activated international assistance and become a major focus for the United Nations. Yet by 1984, rich and poor alike were forced to recognize that development programs had not performed well. It was in that year that Norway's Prime Minister, Gro Harlem Brundtland gave voice to a concept she called "sustainable development", linking programs for economic improvement with the state of the natural environment. This concept had an odd effect, rebounding back on the industrialized world, suggesting that development was as much a problem in the developed nations as it was in those called "developing."

The world quickly embraced the idea of sustainable development, yielding another unexpected outcome. The concept—and its application—had the effect of refocusing attention on the role of education in the complex processes of development.

From its outset, Third World development had included an education component. The guiding perspective was that illiteracy with its links to ignorance – sustains underdevelopment–and that education gives people the private, personal means of improving their economic circumstances. International assistance embarked on a massive effort to eliminate illiteracy on a global basis. Schools were built, teachers were trained, and classes begun in towns and villages on three continents. The education provided by these programs were modelled on that which had proved so successful in the industrialized world. From Bolivia to Botswana, this education offered the standard curriculum—reading and writing, grammar, arithmetic, civics, geography, science.

In time, questions arose as to whether this course of study was appropriate to societies very different from those in which the curriculum had originated. Were these the proper subjects for young people who, upon graduation, would not find jobs waiting for them? The concept of sustainable development raised a new question—could there be an education for development? Should Third World education-curriculum, methods, and philosophy—be modified to point more directly at the development needs of poor countries and more specifically at the need to produce sustainable environments?

Again, these concerns rebounded raising questions about education back home in those countries where the liberating concept of universal schooling had first been applied. Was it possible that the standard curriculum might be out of date? After all, it has persisted without fundamental changes for the last 150 years or so since universal education was established. Teaching methods, too, along with the guiding philosophies of education, had remained more or less the same. In 1995, formal education was still patterned as a classroom experience, just as it was in 1850. Children still sat in rows of desks under the stern, authoritarian eye of the teacher up there in the front of the room. Was this the appropriate education in a world almost totally transformed from what it had been only 150 years ago?

And the questions persisted. Could there be an education for sustainable development? Could there be an education that would yield cultures vitally concerned to protect and defend the planet's resources and its natural environment?

An Essential Instrument

These questions lingered more or less under the surface until the United Nations Conference on the Environment and Development, held in Rio de Janeiro in 1994. At the Rio Summit, the subject of education for development seemed suddenly to come to life. The same questions were being asked on all sides. Can education be shaped to serve as a direct tool of sustainable development? Is it possible that education might help achieve a stable and sustainable environment?

As a result, we, as educators, have found new grounds in seeking to answer these questions. We are saying yes, it is possible that education can help achieve sustainable environments. And we are going further than that. We are saying that education, both formal and informal, will prove to be essential to the achievement of sustainable development. We are suggesting that without the right kind of education, the goal of sustainable development will encounter overwhelming obstacles.

But what is this right kind of education?

Our once reliable system of public education—in the United States and in other developed countries—seem recently to have come up against enormous problems. On a daily basis, we can read in the newspapers that our schools are no longer serving our young people. In the U. S., the dismal performance of many big-city school systems has led to reviews and reconsiderations of every aspect of the educational process. A vast amount of discussion is accompanied by comparatively little change. The idea that education can serve as an essential instrument in the drive toward a bountiful, beautiful and protected environment appears through this haze and clamor like a door opening on a garden. It suggests new roles for education in human life and in the life of our times. Education may be revitalized by its active entrance into these great issues of our time. Already there is some indication that this is exactly what is happening.

New attitudes and ideas inevitably lead to experiments and pockets of experiment in education are now seen to be taking place in many places throughout the world. The industrial world, with its educational problems, is certainly not exempt. The authors are participants in this broad movement. We find ourselves actively engaged in testing

---

Box 1.1. POTENTIAL OF THE KNOWLEDGE-BASED SOCIETY

The advent of a knowledge-based society opens up a promising path to dematerialization, making intensive use of information and skills, rather than natural resources.

A knowledge-based society, emphasizing creativity and diversity can enlarge human choices. Although knowledge is created by private individuals, knowledge is a public good because we can share it without diminishing it.

Three important issues:

First, a knowledge-based society is more than a service economy. In a knowledge-based society typical workers are highly skilled, and their knowledge resides in their brains and life experience, rather than in the machines that they operate.

Second, any restriction on the sharing of knowledge is inefficient, because knowledge can be shared at no cost and can make others better off. But without some restrictions, there may be no incentive to create new knowledge. Solving this paradox of knowledge may require new institutions.

Third, a knowledge-based society is also an information society. An information society requires information infrastructure, encompassing such modes of telecommunications as cable and satellite coverage and telephone lines; computer infrastructure, such as personal computers and the Internet; and social infrastructure, such as educated people and an open society that allows information to flow freely within a society and to and from the rest of the world.

Source: Chichilnisky, Graciela "The knowledge Revolution : Its impact on Consumption Patterns and Resources use." 1997.

new approaches to education for sustainable development here where we work, which happens to be at a state college located within the system of higher education provided by the State of New Jersey.

When you begin to test them, putting in your probes, educational systems begin to look more and more like living entities. Living species evolve and prosper through multiple adaptations rather than by moving along some fixed straight line. Some of those adaptations will work out and become a part of the system while others will wither and die. The Western tradition of education is one of those that has seen its best days and is now withering away. This should be seen as grounds for excitement rather than despair. Rather than narrowly focusing on a Western tradition that has long since hardened and solidified, experimentation is fluidly testing other styles of education—although caution is called for when working with processes that may require generations to achieve results. Nonetheless we can expect that some of these experiments will be successful. And they will not support the exclusionary class structures that have typified the West.

These changes are proceeding alongside tectonic shifts in attitudes toward economic development. The old model— centered on building factories, on transplanting the Western model of the consumer society to other cultures—has largely been abandoned. Development experts have come to the remarkable conclusion that the recipients of development assistance, those who will have to live with the programs, should have some say in what is to be done—that is, if projects are to succeed. The expertise of "the natives" has at last come to be recognized. These shifts have enormous implications for education but they remain largely unrealized. Education, essential as it will prove to be, has not yet begun to play its proper part in the vast panorama of sustainable development.

Changing the educational system to what it should be—in both North and South—is not going to be an easy task. All sorts of resistances have already been encountered—from teachers set in their ways, from school administrators with routine ways of doing things, from educational establishments, from governments and from societies uncomfortable with change.

Opposition and support

What is sustainable development? By one definition it means that the economies of the world must learn to meet the needs of today's generation without compromising or stealing from future generations. One of the things we, as a race, have to realize is that unless we pay very careful attention to the needs of sustainable development, the earth's resources will be depleted and future generations will be bankrupt—not only in debt for what we have borrowed against them, but bankrupt in all of the five major biological systems that support the planet and therefore the economies of the planet. Croplands, forests, grasslands, oceans and fresh water—those are the five. Those are the systems that support the world economy. So whether you're a tribal man in Zimbabwe, who is trying to find a way to maximize his production of corn, or whether you're a corporate CEO who's trying to plot the future of the corporation over time, you both have a common interest in making sure that the world's resources are used so as to guarantee that after your demise future generations will be able to continue what you have begun.

Sustainable development is such an obvious necessity that resistance to it may seem hard to understand. Yet, it is by no means the first clear necessity that the human race has resisted. Some of this resistance can be attributed to ignorance. Education can deal with ignorance, but can it also deal with attitudes? For there are attitudes that refuse to look beyond the short term, attitudes that say, "I'll get mine and the future will take care of itself". Greed is at fault here, and greed finds an ally in inertia, in a devotion to habit and to old ways of doing things.

There are political resistances as well. Governments are seen taking the view that sustainable development exacts a price. What we often hear governments saying is, "Yes, we're all in favor of sustainable development as long as it doesn't impact negatively on our economy". This has its counterpart in personal attitudes, in individuals saying, "Yes, we're very much in favor of sustainable development and of protecting the environment as long as we don't lose our jobs".

And yet for all the opposition, those backing sustainable development have become an accumulative force. As was evident at the Rio Summit, the need for sustainable development has awakened an astonishing and unexpected amount of positive and active support. This is apparent first within the United Nations itself. But it is even more evident among the non-governmental organizations, the private NGOs, which were represented in large numbers in Rio de Janeiro.

There has been a phenomenal growth in NGOs around the world—and in their impact. It is our observation that the NGOs have been more effective in focusing United Nations policies on the critical issues of sustainable development than the member-governments themselves. Indeed, in their separate national settings, NGOs are also a powerful force in dealing with the different governments. Basically, what we and the world are seeing is a grass-roots movement, reflected in the NGOs, that is awakening people everywhere to the great issue of sustainable development.

Yet, for governments—and for all their ambivalence—this issue presents them with opportunities that go far beyond sustainable development itself. It gives governments opportunities to strengthen their grass-roots connections by extending support to local and community organizations. These will often include the very NGOs that have brought the issue to the fore. Governments have never been harmed by reacquainting themselves with the people they rule and represent. And any such reach toward the grass roots will inevitably involve education, but it will be education of a new kind. It will take advantage of the great variety of new technologies that have almost suddenly become available to the governments of the world, technologies that will open the door to a kind of continuing education process in villages in the most remote corners of the world.

To shake people up

This astounding opportunity must circumvent some old fears. If you survey the world scene, you might get the idea that governments, especially governments in developing countries, have some latent fears about the democratization of education. In many of the Third World countries, a belief seems to prevail that if the people become informed, the people will rise up and throw the rascals out. But there is an odd characteristic of these new technologies, one that leaders around the world are going to have to confront. That is that they are almost impossible to suppress and they make it impossible to suppress information. And as long as they are here, with effects impossible to guard against, then there is really only one choice open to governments, that the technologies be used in fruitful and productive ways. What governments should be pressing for, and the United Nations, too, is that these new technologies be used to educate people about the issues of sustainability.

Below governments within the educational setting are the school administrators and teachers and to get them to understand what is required by education for sustainable development, you have to reach them with a set of messages that are entirely new.

Teachers today are not practicing holistic education. Too often, they see teaching as similar to working in a factory, as an earning exercise that shuttles students along to the next grade. But all involved have larger, truer functions to perform. Coca-Cola has to know, whether it wants to or not, that if the corporate exploitation, which for so many years has gone unchecked, continues at its current rate, can only end in its bankruptcy and that of all other corporations. Because all depend on the health of the five biological systems that sustain the world economy.

It cannot be denied that the people of the developing countries have an intuitive awareness of the concept of sustainable development. This somehow has to be developed into a movement that has a political clout. If I am trying to grow cassava on my one hectare plot of land so that I can feed my family and sell the surplus to the people in the village and I know that everyone in the territory around is doing the same thing, I know also that this mode of life cannot continue—as happened in Nigeria—if foreign oil companies are allowed to come in and wreck the land in order to extract its oil, the big cash product. The Nigerian case is an example of how the powerful corporate interests of the developed world team up with local autocrats to annihilate the interests of the local people who are trying to survive in concert with nature. This can only be prevented by grass-roots movements that carry political force.

How the power balance is to be shifted in favor of ordinary men and women is difficult to foresee, but clearly here educational processes are involved. There has to be an organized political effort in many of the developing countries if the rights and the interests of those who are at present powerless are brought to a playing field made level with the rights and interests of the powerful. Such bottom-up movements will involve educational systems that will be put in place only against immense obstacles.

The prospect of the resistance such grass-roots movements will encounter leads us back to the success of the NGO movement because that represents a clear mechanism through which the relatively powerless people of the world are making their case in a legitimate and effective way. This too, was one of the important lessons to be drawn from the Rio Summit. The history of the NGO's is a chronicle of organizations able to make their case so persuasively that it begins to invade and oftentimes prevails in the larger forums, so that governmental policy begins to reflect some of the attitudes coming from the bottom up.

Turning to top-down processes, one becomes instantly aware of the contradiction between what the president of Coca-Cola has to understand and how the oil companies acted in Nigeria. Yet, some of the most powerful figures in the global economy are clearly beginning to rethink their position about exploitation of the natural world. The perils of such exploitation are being brought to their attention via the bottom line—and by their stockholders, board members and outside organizations. The message is that if they continue to take a shortsighted view and exploit for their vested interests, for short-term gains to the detriment of the long term, this will have Draconian implications for the long term in rising and excessive prices for raw materials as well as in the prospect of chaos and disorder. Nobody wants the kind of world that unthinking exploitation will inevitably bring about.

So there are compelling arguments that are being more and more clearly understood by the people on the corporate boards. And sooner or later a response will have to be made to these arguments because of pressures coming from the bottom line and of pressures coming from beneath the bottom line. Mechanisms have emerged that will force the big corporations to change their patterns of behavior. If people begin to believe that a company is doing something that is clearly detrimental to the environment in which these people live, they can simply boycott the product, effecting serious losses in revenue. This, of course, requires organization on the part of the people—and knowledge as well. For them, education will have made the link between the corporation's actions and environmental destruction.

So, there is pressure on corporations to behave themselves. The pressure comes from the top down, which is to say from within and from the bottom up, which is to say usually from without. We have seen such dual pressures working in countries like South Africa. We have seen it in the civil rights movements in the United States. They involve political techniques with which the people of the developing countries are becoming ever more familiar and which they can use to their advantage.

A five-point program

As people begin to be better informed about the specifics of sustainable development, they begin to take positive and proactive positions, both for themselves and for their communities, to ensure that whatever their enterprise is, it is kept linked with a sustained environment. To move further in this direction, a great deal can be done through formal educational processes. A sharpened environmental awareness may not necessarily require the introduction of new curricula into educational systems. And yet education for sustainable development, whether formal or informal, must seek to instill attitudes perhaps even more than transmitting facts. And that calls for an expansion in our concept of what education is and can be.

If we were to draw up a five-point plan, it might look something like this: *First,* we must recognize and encourage the innumerable grass-roots movements working toward sustainable development and be sensitive to the enthusiasm, sensitivity and creativity that these grass-roots movements can bring to bear on the issues. *Second,* we must bring pressure on governments to support educational programs that will ensure that populations are adequately informed. *Third,* we must assist teachers to find new ways to incorporate the issues of sustainable development into the standard subjects. *Fourth,* we must learn to apply new technologies to get enough information to people to enable them to make informed judgements and to take informed political action. And *fifth,* we must find ways to educate teachers and professors to accept their responsibility to develop the whole person. Informed and integrated personalities can be expected to take the political action necessary to sustain the world while helping people emerge from poverty and destitution.

Or we might draw up a program that more directly addresses the problems of education itself. We need to break down the barriers that have been raised between different levels of education. We have this notion that education is compartmentalized into kindergarten, then first through twelfth grades and then college. The truth is that education takes place from the womb to the tomb and we have to understand it as a lifelong process. We have to understand, too, that anyone and everyone can be an educator. And that everyone can and should be educated. Many people already understand that their own comfort, security and well being cannot come at the expense of the comfort, security and well being of others.

We need to do some leapfrogging and take advantage of the technologies that are out there waiting to be tapped. From distance learning and satellite communications to CD-ROM technology, we must make use of these remarkable new techniques which speed up communications and make it easier for everyone to communicate. We need to understand that civility is an important part of the education process, and we need to teach civility and humanity as well as physics and mathematics. We need to realize that there are generational discussions that have to take place—and we are beginning to see that happen.

That the elderly have a role to play in the education of the young––something we are beginning to see a lot of.

Another hopeful sign is that more and more people are interested in discussing the role of education in society. That is a discussion that has been dormant for a long period of time. Education has been seeing itself as not in the forefront of social and human evolution but subservient to the whims of a corporate world and of the economic furnace that provides jobs to graduates. Today, educators are beginning to say again that this is no longer the image they want for themselves. More and more educators are questioning their role in interaction with our economic and financial structures. Out of such questioning we can expect an education for sustainable development to emerge.

Educating the whole person

The seminal idea is that education is not a physical commodity. That it is a vibrant living entity—which nourishes living entities. Like all forms of nourishment, good education nourishes the entire being, while compartmentalized education, like bad food, creates indigestion and generates illness. The failure to nourish the total spirit debilitates society as well as the individual. And as we go on, looking at education as nourishment, as something that we take in that is alive, that is sustaining, we gradually get the feeling that education has to be applied in a much broader and more holistic way. Just as health is a holistic condition. One isn't just healthy mentally or physically, in the liver or in the throat. If one is healthy, one is healthy all over. And we are demanding of education that it play a major role in creating health for individuals as well as for the societies in which those individuals live.

This is where the revolution in education has begun. Our dominant traditions in education are essentially Western. And what those traditions have done is compartmentalize and artificially separate aspects of total education. The Western tradition has made it easy to say that all we have to do is work on the intellectual development of the human being—as though the moral, ethical and spiritual elements were not important. When those aspects of being human are dropped from the curriculum, educational systems are created that artificially focus on just one aspect of the total human being.

What we are beginning to see today is the return of moral and ethical considerations into higher education, the arena in which the authors conduct their daily labors. So far, it is only a preliminary thrust and we believe that much more attention needs to be given—and will be given—to ethics and morals. And not only in terms of how the students view themselves as moral and ethical beings but who will soon take an active part in the larger community. Equally important is the question of what are the moral and ethical values that will sustain the society to which students belong. The answers to such questions come from moral and ethical understanding.

What we need to do is learn from horrible past examples, of which we have a wide variety to choose from. The brightest people in the world can come out of the best intellectual training in the world only to create horrendous tragedy because they lacked moral and ethical development. They had no sense of the totality of the spirit. The kind of education we need is an education that will free itself from the confines of the campus and go out to meet people where they live and work, where they have children and where they have crises, where they get married and live their lives. An education that is tied to the everyday life of people will be the education that will bring all of these pieces together.

The intellect is just a small part of the full human being. And yet in Western culture we have spent 99 per cent of our resources on trying to develop that one small part while forgetting about the rest of the beast. This is the system that has to be turned around. We need a system that will help create a sustainable environment for everyone. We need education that understands that there are moral and ethical imperatives, one of which is that we must sustain this beautiful and fruitful planet that is both our greatest gift and our precious home.

Reaching out—to the ends of the Earth

This kind of education need not occur only within the confines of educational institutions. There are great moralists and there are great ethical thinkers who are plowing fields, who are working with children, who may not even have formal education, but whose life experiences are such that they have in fact developed excellent ethical and moral systems for the planet. We believe that the revolution will come—and is coming—in the technology that is allowing people to come together in ways they could not have come together in the past. Technology is a vehicle and as such cannot be separated from the educational revolution in which it is beginning to play a part. Computer-based distance learning allows people to interact over thousands of miles regardless of what their habitats are like and how different their societies might be. People are beginning to understand each other's lives in ways that they could never have done before. There is a revolution occurring below the surface, whether we are aware of it or not.

Distance learning is a new technology that needs to be examined in detail. It shatters the notion that the classroom is the be-all and end-all of the educational process. One can establish a wonderful series of learning experiences via the electronic media, our thoughts beamed to the most remote places of the world. And those remote places can then beam their information and opinions back to us. Equally important are the new CD-ROM technologies, which stand on the edge of a vast expansion. CD-ROM facilitates the presentation of subject matter in an interactive way which catches the students' interest and stimulates their thinking. These technologies, applied to the third world, will take us far beyond the narrow goal of eradicating illiteracy.

We need to break the attitude that literacy alone constitutes the sum-total of educational accomplishment. Literacy should be seen as one more tool to be applied for the greater good of humanity. What we have done with our literacy programs, packed along as they were in the broader program for Third World development, is to take a very Western approach by looking to literacy as a short-term answer to development problems. The experts said okay, let us make everyone literate. But that, in and of itself, fails to accomplish anything. Literacy has to have its own goals and purposes. And this calls for methods and attitudes that go beyond literacy. The new technologies open up this field enabling us to approach the contextual issues of literacy in ways that would have been impossible in the past.

So we have these new electronic technologies that allow us to interact—with the machine and with the farthest reaches of our planet. There are the new political technologies for breaking down the barriers of inertia and opposition. New pedagogical technologies say that college exists everywhere. That you can teach in a church, that you can teach in a storeroom, that you can teach on a street corner. And that the teachers must go to where the people are rather than insisting that the people come to where the teachers are. That is a methodology in and of itself. In itself it constitutes a whole technology. It is a political technology that is beginning to take hold and which will have, as one of its outcomes, a global movement towards sustainable development.

We have inherited an educational system that unfortunately keeps most people under the yoke, so to speak, of special interests. And we have built educational dogmas and philosophies that almost make that seem reasonable. It is a system which engenders the belief that not every one can share in health and in social and psychological well being. And that what we must have is a situation in which only some people can take advantage of what the planet has to offer. It is a very Western approach. It is a very attitudinal approach. It is a class-conscious approach to the sustainable environment. What we need to do is create an educational system in which we can use current technology to bring people to a level of literacy and information at which they can question those basic assumptions.

And we must do this quickly. Because it is through education that people will come to question those very erroneous assumptions about how human beings interact with one another and ultimately how they interact with the planet. One way to do that, we believe as college administrators, is to break down the barriers that currently lock in the way we provide education. We don't believe that an education has to be provided in a certain building or in a specific setting. We think education must go to where the people live. It must go out into the world.

Education, the key

The Earth Summit in Rio was for us a life–transforming experience. And by that we mean it educated us not just in terms of ideas. It brought about a fundamental shift in our attitude toward what we need to do to help create a literate world and a sustainable environment. We wish the 35,000 people in Rio could have been 350,000. We wish it had been three-and-a-half millions. What we took with us from the Earth Summit was a sense that there are thousands of people, millions of people, who are now beginning to realize that society must change and that the educational system, if it is going to have a significant role to play in society, must change along with it.

We can no longer look at literacy, for example, as something achieved for its own sake. Literacy must be viewed as a tool to allow people critically to question the assumptions they have been given, the philosophies and dogmas that have been fed by a very select group who want the majority of people to believe that the status quo is the natural order of the world. And we think what we experienced at the Earth Summit and again at the Social Summit in Copenhagen was a fundamental shift in how a significant number of people are beginning to think about education. They are coming to understand that it can and should be life-transforming.

They are coming to understand that it will ultimately impact upon people's attitudes—not just about themselves but about how they relate to one another in a global perspective. In this sense, education is the key. And it becomes a significant key that unlocks a variety of remedies and solutions.

····

Earth and Humans

Rashmi Mayur

There is a crime here which goes beyond denunciation.
There is a sorrow here that weeping cannot symbolize.
There is a failure here that topples all our success.
— *John Steinbeck*

Each day, everywhere, humans – one of the more than forty million species of life on this tiny spaceship – must rediscover their original relationship with the forgotten planet. Humans are products of more than 4 billion years of evolution of life; they live for a miniscule moment of time and disappear as all the other creatures do. During the last 4 billion years that Man has been on this unique, rich and beautiful planet, everything living and non-living has coexisted in harmony. Some species survived, many became extinct but evolution has continued relentlessly.

Almost 150 million years ago, great dinosaurs ruled the Earth. They were invincible, but suddenly because of mysterious combinations of conditions, they disappeared around 60 million years ago. Man, now, controls the destiny of this tiny solar satellite. What is happening to this only "home" we have is apocalyptic. The ecological state of our earth is in disarray and it is worsening day by day. The process of destruction of the environment has been going on for more than four hundred years as a consequence of the industrial technological revolution. We do not know when and how this devastation will end.

In this age of "progress" and "development" there are worldwide attempts to cast the Earth in the image of the humans as if the Earth is human property. If, in the process, what was created through evolution before industrialization began is eliminated or destroyed, that is of very little or no concern for the "modernizers" or "developers".

Box 2.1. **THE SPIRAL OF LIFE**

Life creates life—a puzzle and a paradox. Left undisturbed, forms of life reproduce themselves and multiply, creating a stunning variety of species and natural communities. When the first European settlers arrived in the New World about 400 years ago, they encountered an untamed wilderness busily engaged in this ancient task of making and remaking life. The settlers immediately began to tame the land, making it useful for fulfilling human needs. And everywhere they went, they interrupted and modified the processes that had generated, over millennia, life's great diversity of form.

Only later did a few visionaries begin to worry that they were destroying something of value. Gradually the idea emerged that communities of life and the processes that formed them have irreplaceable value; over time, a system of forests, parks, refuges, and wilderness areas was set aside; Paul Ehrlich, an eminent biologist notes, that these are our last best hope of preserving the biodiversity— necessary to a viable future. The power of the creative force, biologists call "adaptation and natural selection" is exhibited in all these areas: in a remnant of the great tropical moist forest that once covered Puerto Rico and in an oasis in the Mojave desert; in tiny patches of tall-grass prairie remaining in the Midwest and in old-growth forests of the northern Pacific Coast; in all of these and dozens more, one can see the multiple versions of life's creativity.

The native American cultures—the first peoples of the continent who are now being displaced—could have told the new people what they were losing, had anyone been willing to listen. They could have learned, for instance, what Brave Buffalo, a Sioux, had learned as a child:

"When I was ten years of age I looked at the land and the rivers, the sky above, and the animals around me and could not fail to realize that they were made by some great power. I was so anxious to understand this power that I questioned the trees and the bushes. It seemed as though the flowers were staring at me, and I wanted to ask them : Who made you?" I looked at the moss-covered stones... but they could not answer me. Then I had a dream, and in my dream one of these small round stones appeared to me and told me that the maker of all *was Wakan tanka,* and in order to honor him I must honor the works in nature".

Source : *"The world of Wilderness",* edited by T.H.Watkins and Patricia Byrnes, (The spiral of life, *Bryan. G. Norton* with extracts from its introduction), p 35, 1995.

In its primeval state, Nature exists in the wilderness where the living and non-living elements establish symbiotically harmonious relationships. In the universe, nothing is static; as Buddha says, change is the immutable principle of existence. The wilderness has its own beauty and it bestows joy, freedom and creativity.

Humans on the other hand, it seems, have alienated from the natural processes on another planet independent of all other forms of life. For nature time is infinite. For humans it is finite. Their unique characteristic, that is intelligence, is also finite. It cannot comprehend the long-term implications of incarcerating Nature and disrupting millions of years of its handiwork. That is why the destruction of the rainforests, the extinction of innumerable species, the systematic plundering of rivers and oceans, the pollution of air and soils and the annihilation of almost every natural system, have become callous acts of global ignominy. We consume endlessly —at any cost. Technology brings new products and goods, and the media reaches our gullible masses subliminally, converting the superfluous into the essential.

For many scientist/thinkers in the last century, and even today, the Industrial Revolution heralded the coming of utopia— the dreamworld for which humanity has been hoping for perhaps all of history. Science systematically acquired knowledge about the working of the physical, chemical and biological world and the application of this knowledge by developing technology became the cornerstone of the new era— the era of development. In many of the poorer countries, in their yearning for industrialization, the mantra is 'development at any cost'. You are charged with being primitivist if you challenge that dictum. You are not supposed to ask questions such as: "Industrialization for whom? Industrialization at what cost? What are the implications of industrialization for human society? What are its consequences on the total biological and physical systems of the earth? Where is this rampant unrestrained development taking us?"

The Earth is under siege by us. We have been transformed into insatiable consumers. The issue before the Eskimos is not whether they need refrigerators, but how they can buy them and use them. For most humans, consumption is the central purpose of life.

The world has been converted into a marketplace, a place where we sell goods and services, a place where even miseries are bought and sold, a place for self-gratification, a place where the only things that count in our existence are material things––automobiles, televisions, videos, air conditioners, highways, factories, banks, guns, and the endless number of gadgets churned out interminably to meet the multiplying demands—demands aroused in more and more people insatiably. In this process, which is learning without questioning, wants are converted into needs, and what is truly needed is ignored. For example, a hungry child in Nairobi spends many hours watching TV. As the demands proliferate, the resources at the local and the global level needed to meet the secondary and tertiary wants, shrink as also the ecological systems deteriorate. In time, as is evident worldwide, increasing numbers of people, live in the state of depravation.

The assumptions on which the technological civilization is based—that the resources are unlimited and that the technologies can solve all the problems—lead us to the conclusion that Nature will continue to supply resources forever. If, in the process, the millennial rainforests are cut down along with all the treasures, which have taken millions of years to accumulate, well, that simply does not matter. If ozone is depleted, if climate changes, if millions of species are driven to extinction, if the oceans die and the soils are poisoned or eroded—that is no more than the price we must pay for the industrial civilization, which is considered sacred, but, which, in fact, is a man-made 'air-conditioned nightmare', as Henry Miller, a great writer, once despaired.

Any intelligent person can witness the ravages inflicted on the earth because of the erroneous philosophy which has guided our developments during the last 200 years. When the first report of the Club of Rome, the Limits to Growth, was released during the early seventies, to many arrogant developmentalists, it was a threat. They branded it as a 'document of doom'. Within a decade, President Carter of the United States directed the Council on Environmental Quality to prepare the Global 2000 report recognizing that the future of humanity was at stake. A monumental study, which was released in 1980, warned of the threats facing humanity, as Gerard O.Barney, the Study Director declared, "if very real problems are ignored." The falseties of the premises on which the present human civilization is based are clearly evident, requiring the fundamental changes in the direction of our civilization. Even after 19 years, despite all the limitations of these reports, their projections remain valid.

Never before in human history have people from all over the world and from every walk of life discussed, shared, argued and prepared a final report —the Agenda 21 —at the Earth Summit in June 1992, in Rio de Janeiro, Brazil. With all its limitations, it is a primary book for us to study. It was a charter of hope. It has been bellied by the ruthless march of the failed civilization. Most people in the world are either ignorant or oblivious or paralyzed or living in denials while the advance towards doomsday continues. Common sense tells us that we cannot have unlimited number of people when the resources are limited.

Our concern is to change the society by bringing the knowledge we have accumulated during the last several decades to the people everywhere. People must know and having known, they must change the reality. During the last three centuries, the educational systems were designed to build and perpetuate the technological and human systems based on exploitation. Everywhere, people have submitted, uncritically to the monolithic, dehumanized, steel, cement and concrete civilization. It is an anthropocentric civilization taking us fatalistically to an end.

There are many who refuse to accept the doom. Groups and individuals who are challenging the system exist all over the world at a grassroots, regional and even global level. Some of them are: Rain forest Action Committee, *Chipko* movement to save forests in India, Green party in Germany, Green development movement in Kenya, etc. They care for the future and understand the fundamental values of life and the earth. They challenge the arrogance of humans. They are seeking earth knowledge —the knowledge, which will help to challenge the environmentally harmful projects and assist us to harmonize with the society as a whole and with nature. They refuse to be enslaved by the consumer society. They denounce the philosophy of a lifetime spent on superfluous production and unlimited consumption to fulfill pseudo needs.

The task confronting us is not easy. Those of us who are privileged have been paralyzed in the name of false security, but as we discovered at the UN meeting, 'Rio Plus-five', by failing to revolt against the forces of perpetuation, we continue to move towards the 'Rio minus'.

Life is a process of creativity. In humans, it is through learning that we develop and find purposes, by pursuing which we realize our dreams. For a long time we have lived in a tunnel of darkness. Now, our task is to release all our creative powers by developing a global movement for protecting the earth and bringing joy and happiness to every creature sharing the bounties of Nature.

....

Can the Human Race Survive the Human Race?

Daniel D. Chiras

The basis for optimism is sheer terror.
— *Oscar Wilde*

If this is a typical day on planet Earth, 116 square miles of tropical rain forest will be destroyed. In the Third World, where much of the cutting occurs, only one tree is planted for every ten cut down; in the tropics of Africa, the ratio is one to 29.

If this is a typical day, 72 square miles of desert will form in semi arid regions subject to intense population pressure, overgrazing, and poor land management. Already, one-third of the world's cropland is threatened by desertification.

As if that is not bad enough, today 250,000 newborns will join the world population. Each new resident requires food, water, shelter, and a host of other resources to survive.

On this day, at least 1.5 million tons of hazardous waste will be "disposed of"—released into our air, water, and land—and Americans will throw away enough garbage to fill the Superdome in New Orleans two times. By various estimates, 40 to 100 species will become extinct today, mostly as the result of tropical deforestation.

At day's end, the Earth will be a little hotter, the rain a little more acidic and the water a little more polluted. The world's already crowded cities will be more crowded and the air in and around them, now choked with pollution, will be a bit dirtier. At day's end, the web of life will be a bit more threadbare.

Tomorrow, it starts all over again.

A survey of global environmental problems suggests what

many have feared for some time now: the fate of the Earth and our own survival are on the line. The next ten years could determine the future of humankind. It's time to mobilize, to save the Earth and save ourselves. There's no better place to start than with agriculture.

Soil erosion is destroying cropland and rangeland throughout the world. In the past 100 years, one-third of the topsoil on American farms has been stripped from the land by wind and rain. Each year, nearly two billion tons of soil is blown off or washed away from farms and ranches. If this trend continues, U.S. crop production could decline by 10 to 30 percent in the next 50 years, a time when world demand for food and alternative fuels from crops, like ethanol, is on the rise.

Unfortunately, Americans are not alone in their plight. Worldwide, an estimated 24 billion tons of topsoil is eroded from farms and ranches each year. If this soil could be captured, it would fill a freight train that could encircle the equator 170 times.

The loss of topsoil is important because it destroys farmland. At the current rate of loss, 7 percent of the world's cropland will be forfeited to erosion in the next ten years. Making matters worse, valuable cropland and rangeland are also being destroyed by other forces such as the spread of desert and cropland conversion—the loss of arable land to airports, highways, housing developments and so forth.

Hunger and starvation exist in epidemic proportions and are likely to worsen as the human population expands. Despite three decades of agricultural research to increase the world's food supply, one of every five Third World inhabitants cannot find enough to eat. They are literally starving to death. Worldwide, 12 million people will succumb to starvation this year, and 30 million more will perish from diseases aggravated by hunger. Forty-two million people dying each year is equivalent to 300

Boeing 747s, each carrying 400 passengers, crashing every day of the year with no survivors. Almost half of the victims are children.

Although efforts to feed the world's people are impressive, hunger and starvation are likely to worsen as the world population swells. In addition to these problems, continued growth of the human population could double or even triple deforestation and other environmental damage already occurring at intolerable levels today. It won't be long before we have eaten ourselves out of house and home.

Rapid deforestation threatens the long-term ecological stability of the planet. Rain forests are a rich source of diverse wild species, new medicines, and useful products. Once covering an area the size of the United States, tropical rain forests have been reduced by at least a third, perhaps as much as a half. In some areas, deforestation has nearly wiped out the forests. The forests of the island nations of Borneo and Sumatra, for example, have been nearly decimated. Forty years ago Ethiopia was 30 percent forest;12 years ago, only 4 percent of the nation was covered with trees, and today it is less than 1 percent. Before the turn of the century, India was 50 percent forest; today about 14 percent of the area is covered with trees.

Oil supplies could be depleted by the year 2018 if oil consumption continues to increase at current rates. The industrial world depends heavily on oil. At the current rate of consumption, however, known world oil supplies will only last about 40 more years. Undiscovered oil—that is, oil thought to exist—might last for another 25 years. Unfortunately, oil consumption has increased at a rate of 5 percent a year since its discovery. If demand continues to increase this quickly, world oil reserves could be depleted by 2018. Some geologists in the oil industry believe that global oil supplies are much larger than those currently thought to exist (about 1,400 billion barrels).

It is possible, they say, that an additional 3,000 billion barrels of oils could be had. Although this is a massive amount, a quick calculation, taking into account a 5 percent annual growth in demand

---

Box 3.1. RAIN FORESTS

Rainforests cover less than two percent of the Earth's surface, yet they are home to some 50 to 70 percent of all life forms on our planet. The rainforests are the richest, oldest, most productive and most complex ecosystems on Earth. As biologist Norman Myers notes, "Rainforests are the finest celebration of nature ever known on the planet." And never before has nature's greatest orchestration been so threatened.

Global Rates of Destruction

— 2.47 acres (1 hectare) per second: equivalent to two U.S. football fields

— 150 acres (60 hectares) per minute

— 214,000 acres (86,000 hectares) per day: an area larger than New York City

— 78 million acres (31 million hectares) per year: an area larger than Poland

In Brazil:

— 5.4 million acres per year (estimate averaged for period 1979-1990)

— 6-9 million indigenous people inhabited the Brazilian rainforest in the year 1500 AD. In 1992, less than 200,000 remained.

Species Extinction

Distinguished scientists estimate an average of 137 species of life forms are driven into extinction every day, or 50,000 each year.

Why rainforests are important

Tropical rainforests are by far the richest habitat on Earth. As many as 30 million species of plants and animals - more than half of all life forms - live in tropical rainforests. At least two-thirds of the world's plant species, including many exotic and beautiful flowers, as well as plants with medicinal value, occur in the tropics and subtropics.

Rainforests are part of the global weather system. Destroying them alters the hydrological cycle — causing drought, flooding, and soil erosion in areas where such events were previously rare. The cutting of forests

reveals that even this seemingly vast supply will only last an additional 20 years. By 2038, that is, the world could be completely out of oil.

also changes the albedo or reflectivity of the earth's surface, which in turn alters wind and ocean current patterns, and changes rainfall distribution.

Threat to the Amazon

As the largest rainforest on Earth—spanning nine countries, containing one-fifth of the world's fresh water, and a third of the known living species—the Amazon Basin is a global treasure. Encompassing an area the size of the continental United States, the Amazon is home to hundreds of indigenous groups, all with distinct cultures evolved over the millennia in harmony with the region's vibrant rainforest ecosystems.

However, times are changing—and so will the Amazon. With recent political repositioning throughout South America, the Amazon Basin is quickly moving to the forefront of international economic and political interests. Fueled by potential trade profits, governments in the region have entered into a series of cooperative trade agreements (Andean Pact, Mercosur, and others) to forge new economic and geographic links between nations. New transportation routes are a critical component of government plans to move trade forward. Many infrastructure blueprints from earlier decades—including plans to criss-cross the region with highways and dredge-key waterways to access the Amazon's abundant natural resources for commercial trade—are back in discussion and planning.

If these international projects—from hydroelectric dams to oil pipelines—go forward, they will change forever the ecological, economic and social face of the Amazon Basin. New regions and cultures will be rushed into the already developed areas of South America at an unprecedented pace. With the legacy of environmental devastation and genocide resulting from earlier development schemes in the Amazon, concerned observers seriously question government and industry claims that the basin's fragile ecosystems and native peoples will be protected as these projects move forward.

Source :The Rainforest Action Network, San Francisco, CA 94111 415-398-4404-P; 415-398-2732-F,email: lianas@igc.apc.org

Without carefully developed alternatives, the decline in oil supplies could spawn an inflationary spiral that would cripple the industrialized world. Unfortunately, in many countries relatively little effort is currently being made to use oil more efficiently. Even less effort is focused on developing environmentally safe alternatives, such as hydrogen, ethanol, and solar energy.

Many crucial minerals are bound to fall into short supply in the near future. Current estimates of world mineral reserves and projections of consumption suggest that about three-quarters of the 80 or so economically vital minerals are abundant enough to meet our needs for many years—or, if they are not, there are adequate substitutes available. However, at least 18 economically essential minerals—gold, silver, mercury, lead, sulfur, tin, tungsten, and zinc among them—will fall into short supply, some within a decade or two. Shortages will occur even if nations greatly increase recovery and recycling.

Box 3.2. TAKES 2.8 TONS OF ORE TO FIND ENOUGH GOLD FOR 1 RING

In his cover story on gold mining, Dennis Cauchon marvels at modern-day mining technologies that enables miners to remove "invisible specks of gold" from rock ("The New Gold Rush").

Today's gold miners can remove "amounts as small as one ounce of gold for every 33 tons of rock," he writes, and still make a profit. But Cauchon correctly notes that this current "gold boom" is subsidized by a "controversial 1872 law that basically gives government land to anyone who can prove a valuable discovery." In fact, since 1994 the US government has given away to large mining companies more than $15 billion worth of minerals.

Unfortunately, Cauchon dedicates only two sentences to the long-term environmental impact caused by large-scale gold mining operations. "Environmental regulations have softened the scarring that strip-mining does to the land," he writes.

Don't count on new discoveries and improved extraction technologies to save the day. Even if we could mine five times the currently known reserves of these 18 endangered minerals, they would be 80 percent depleted on or before the year 2040. Their depletion, combined with declining oil supplies, could bring the world economy to its knees—unless we make significant changes in consumption, and soon.

Acid rain and snow are destroying lakes, rivers, forests, and farmland. Today, over 230 lakes in the Adirondack Mountains of New York have become critically acidified from sulfuric and nitric acids, produced from sulfur dioxide and nitrogen oxides released by the combustion of fossil fuels. In lakes and rivers, acids kill fish, algae, and aquatic plants. In 1988, the National Wildlife Federation published a list of U.S. lakes that have high acid levels or are sensitive to acid precipitation. The report adds that one-third of the lakes in Florida are acidic enough to be harmful to aquatic life.

In reality, modern-day gold mining has devastating consequences. Open pits and waste-rock piles have permanently scarred the landscape. Toxic waste from active mine sites contaminates our surface and ground water resources, threatening wildlife habitat as well as local drinking water supplies. And weak regulations and lax enforcement allow irresponsible miners to continue mining.

And why all this devastation? What is gold's primary purpose? Jewelry. Jewelry fabrication accounted for 84% of worldwide gold consumption in 1995. In fact more than 2.8 tons of ore are required to produce one simple gold ring.

It is time for Congress to pass comprehensive mining-law reform to address the fiscal and environmental abuses of the 1872 Mining Law so that taxpayers can share in these profits and future generations can experience the beauty of this country.

Source : Letters to the editor, Washington Post. Stephen D'Esposito, Vice Pres; Mineral Policy Center, Washington. D.C

Throughout much of the developed world, the story is the same. In Southern Sweden, 20,000 lakes are without or some think soon to be, without fish, in large parts because of widespread acidification. In Canada, the prospects for lakes and rivers are also dimming. Nine of Nova Scotia's famous salmon-fishing rivers have already lost their fish populations because of acids deposited in rain and snow. Eleven more are teetering on the brink of destruction. In southern Ontario and Quebec, acid deposition has already destroyed 100 lakes, and by the year 2000, scientists predict, nearly half of Quebec's 48,000 lakes will be destroyed.

Hazardous waste continues to be dumped in the environment. Each year, American factories produce an estimated 250 to 270 million metric tons of waste considered hazardous by State and Federal standards. That's over a ton of hazardous waste each year for every man, woman, and child in the United States. Despite tighter regulations and concerted efforts to reduce the generation of hazardous waste, a lot of toxic chemicals still end up in our groundwater, rivers, lakes, and landfills. Other industrial nations produce equally impressive amounts of hazardous waste. It is unlikely that the world can continue to absorb such an enormous output of waste without creating massive problems in the long run.

Greenhouse gases and deforestation are causing the planet to heat up. Addicted to fossil fuels, modern industrial nations may well be setting the stage for a disastrous global warming. Global warming results from at least three atmospheric pollutants: carbon dioxide, methane, and chloroflurocarbons, all produced by modern industrial societies. These gases absorb heat escaping from the Earth's surface and radiate it back to us, much like the glass in a greenhouse.

Global atmospheric levels of carbon dioxide have increased 25 per cent since 1870 as a result of increased fossil fuel

Box 3.3. ACID RAIN

The only place on earth where pure water is found is in a laboratory. Rain water always contains small amounts of impurities. These impurities come from dust particles or are absorbed from the gases in the air. If pure water is exposed to the air it absorbs carbon dioxide to form carbonic acid and becomes slightly acidic, dropping from pH 7 i.e. neutral, to pH 5.6. Even in remote, unpopulated areas rain can reach a pH of 4.5. However, a pH of less than 4.5 in rain is almost certainly caused by pollution.

Acid rain is caused by the release of the gases SO_2 (sulphur dioxide) and NOX (nitrous oxides). The main sources of SO_2 in the air are coal-fired power stations and metal working industries. The main sources of NOX emissions are vehicles and fuel combustion. SO_2 reacts with water vapour and sunlight to form sulphuric acid. Likewise NOX form nitric acid in the air. These reactions takes hours, or even days, during which polluted air may move hundreds of kilometers. Thus acid rain can fall far from the source of pollution.

When mist or fog droplets condense, they remove pollutants from the air and can become more strongly acidic than acid rain. Even snow can be acid. Gases and particles, not dissolved in water, with a low pH can also be deposited directly onto soil, grass and leaves. It is possible that even more acidity is deposited in this way than by rain! Not much is known about this process, and it is particularly difficult to study.

Acid rain can increase the acidity of lakes, dams and streams and cause the death of aquatic life. Acid rain can increase the acidity of soil, water and shallow groundwater. Acid rain has been linked with the death of trees in Europe and North America. In spite of a great deal of research, no one yet knows exactly how acid rain harms forests.

It seems that the slow-growing, longer lived forests of the North may be more susceptible than the faster growing, shorter lived forests of South Africa. Acid rain erodes buildings and monuments. Acid particles in the air are suspected of contributing to respiratory problems in people.

The effects of acid rain started showing up in the 1970s. Fish were washing up along the beaches, and the term "wet desert" was being used to describe the clear, fishless lakes. For example, the Canadian province of Ontario now has over 100 fishless and acidified lakes. Many types of species such as the lake trout, the wall-eye, burbot and the

Smallmouth bass have nearly vanished from most of these lakes. Starting in 1981, over 200 lakes were monitored in Ontario, Quebec and the Atlantic Provinces, and in 1994, 33% showed some marked improvement in acidity while over 10% were worse. The remaining 56% had at least stable acidity levels.

A very highly publicized problem is the effect of acid rain on trees. Conifers appear to be particularly affected, with needles dropping off, and seedlings failing to produce new trees. The acid also reacts with many nutrients the tree needs, such as calcium, magnesium and potassium, which starves the trees.

Rather surprisingly, the effects of acid rain on trees have overshadowed the effects on people. Many toxic metals are held in the ground in compounds. However, acid rain can breakdown some of these compounds, freeing these metals and washing them into water sources such as rivers. In Sweden, nearly 10,000 lakes now have such high mercury concentrations that people are advised not to eat fish caught in them. As the water becomes more acidic, it can also react with lead and copper water pipes, contaminating drinking water supplies. In Sweden, drinking water reached a stage where it contained enough copper to turn your hair green.

What can we do?

No simple overnight solution is possible. We need to use energy more efficiently at home, in our vehicles and in industry.

The best approach to acid rain is to reduce the amount of NOX and SO_2 being released into the atmosphere. Fitting a catalytic converter to cars can reduce the emissions of NOX by up to 90 percent, but they are very expensive, and cause more carbon dioxide to be released, which contributes to the greenhouse effect.

SO_2 emissions from power stations can be reduced before, during, or after combustion. If a fuel with a low sulphur content (such as North Sea gas or oil) is burned, not much sulphur dioxide will be formed.

Another option is not to burn fossil fuels, but to use alternative energy sources.

You can help in lots of ways:

— Turn off lights when you leave a room.
— If you have a car, don't use it for short journeys.
— Insulate your house properly.
— Basically, anything at all that uses less energy.

combustion and deforestation. Scientists predict that global carbon dioxide levels could double in the next 400 years, raising average global temperature by 4 to 9°F. A decrease in global temperature of only a few degrees means the difference between an ice age and today's relatively livable global climate. A 4 to 9°F increase would have devastating effects. Much of the United States and Canada would be warmer and drier. The agriculturally productive Great Plain States could very likely become too arid to support farming. The United States and Canada, both major exporters of food, might face severe food shortages.

Global warming could eventually melt the polar ice caps and many of the world's glaciers, raising the sea level by as much as 200 to 300 feet and flooding 20 percent of the world's landmass. Much of the state of Florida and many coastal cities throughout the world would be under water. Without an extensive system of levees to hold back rising seas, New York and Los Angeles would cease to exist. Farmland, already threatened by lower rainfall and searing temperatures, would shrink as displaced coastal residents move inland to avoid the rising seas.

Signs of global warming are already evident. In fact, seven of the hottest years in over a century of record keeping have occurred since 1980. If the temperature continues to rise as it has in the past 20 years, the Earth will soon be warmer than it has been in the last 100,000 years.

The trends in environmental deterioration and resource depletion paint a rather ominous picture of the present state of affairs. Lest we forget, many of the changes currently underway could act synergistically, producing far greater damage than anticipated.

Taken together, these trends point to one inescapable conclusion: the current course of human society is unsustainable. It cannot continue much longer the way it has for the past 200 years.

Box 3.4. **MINAMATA DISEASE**

In the early 1950s, people in the small coastal village of Minamata, Japan, noticed strange behavior that they called dancing cats. Inexplicably, cats would begin twitching and stumbling about as if they were drunk. Many became "suicidal" and staggered off docks into the ocean. It was an ominous warning. Their cats were suffering from brain damage that we now know was caused by methyl mercury poisoning.

In 1956, the first human case of neurological damage was reported. A five-year-old girl who had suddenly lapsed into a convulsive delirium was brought into the local clinic. Within a few weeks there seemed to be an epidemic of nervous problems in the village, including numbness, tingling sensations, headaches, blurred vision, slurred speech and loss of muscle control. For an unlucky few, these milder symptoms were followed by violent trembling, paralysis and even death. An abnormally high rate of birth defects also occurred. Children were born with tragic deformities, paralysis and permanent mental retardation. Lengthy investigations showed that these symptoms were caused by mercury from fish and seafood that formed a major part of the diet of both humans and their cats.

For years, the Chisso Chemical Plant had been releasing residues containing mercury into Minamata Bay. Since elemental mercury is not water soluble, it was assumed that it would sink into the bottom sediments and remain inert. Scientists discovered, however, that bacteria living in the sediments were able to convert metallic mercury into soluble methyl mercury, which was absorbed from the water and concentrated in the tissues of aquatic organisms. People who ate fish and shellfish from the bay were exposed to dangerously high levels of this toxic chemical. Altogether, more than 3,500 people were affected and about 50 died of what became known as Minamata Disease. After nearly twenty years of rancorous protests and litigation, the Chisso Company finally admitted that it was guilty of dumping the mercury and agreed to pay reparations to the victims.

Dumping of mercury into Minamata Bay was stopped twenty years ago. Mud containing mercury was dredged up and buried elsewhere so the bay is now considered safe for fishing. The minds and bodies of those people who ate the mercury-poisoned fish, however, can never be repaired. Have we learned from this tragedy how to anticipate and prevent future environmental disasters?

Overshooting the Earth's Carrying Capacity

What's happening on planet Earth? From an ecological perspective, human society has slowly and inexorably pushed beyond the means of the earth's life support system. The massive multibillion dollar human economy is destroying the intricate economy of nature, which unknown to many, is not just the source of human wealth but also the source of all life.

In the language of ecologists, humans have exceeded the earth's carrying capacity. The environmental problems we face are signs that we have transgressed critical ecological thresholds. Unfortunately, few people in positions of power understand the meaning of carrying capacity and the limits it places on human endeavor. Even fewer, understand how far we have overstepped ecological boundaries and the long-term consequences of continuing to do so. An understanding of the term 'carrying capacity' is therefore vital to solving our problems.

Carrying capacity does indeed refer to the ability of our environment to provide food and living space, but the term also encompasses at least two additional factors: resource supply and waste assimilation.

Consider resource supply first. Modern society requires many resources. In industrial nations, economies depend chiefly on our ability to draw sustenance from a finite natural world—that is, from nonrenewable resources such as oil, natural gas, and minerals. Given trends in population growth, nonrenewable resource supplies, and demand, our continued existence will depend on our ability to shift from finite non-renewable resources to renewable resources. This includes wind, hydropower, solar energy, forests, and crops. Today's challenge, then, is to refrain from destroying forests, grasslands, and other resources that can provide a continuous supply of food and materials, and to rebuild

Box 3.5. SMOG AND HEALTH

The symptoms are familiar to all those who live in cities where the air is polluted: aching lungs, wheezing, coughing, headache. Millions of residents of the U.S. South Coast Basin (which includes Los Angeles) breathe dirty air one day of every three.

Ozone levels here, or what most refer to as smog, are often twice the U.S. government health standard.

What does all of this polluted air do to the body? The answer depends on the situation. How long a person is exposed to pollution, the type and concentration, the place, time and day, temperature, weather and more. But one thing is certain: Smog is harmful to your health.

Lungs are ozone's primary target. Studies on animals show that ozone damages cells in the lung's airways, causing inflammation and swelling. It also reduces the respiratory system's ability to fight infection and remove foreign particles.

Ozone may pose a particular health threat to those who already suffer from respiratory problems such as asthma, emphysema and chronic bronchitis. About 10% of the Basin's approximately 14 million residents fit into this category. Ozone may also pose a health threat to the young, elderly, and cardiovascular patients.

Ozone affects healthy people as well. In 1990, California's State Air Resources Board established a new health advisory level in response to mounting evidence that smog affects healthy, exercising adults at lower levels than previously believed. Now, a health advisory is issued at .15 parts per million (on the pollutant standards index) before a first stage smog alert is called when ozone levels reach .20 ppm.

During a health advisory, everyone, including healthy adults and children are advised to avoid prolonged, vigorous outdoor exercise. Susceptible individuals, including those with heart or lung disease, should avoid outdoor activities until the advisory is cancelled. Currently, the U.S. government is reviewing the adequacy of the federal health standard for ozone and is considering tightening it.

Sources of Smog

The sources of pollution include emissions from on-road vehicles, non-road vehicles like planes, ships and trains, industries, and even small businesses and households where polluting products are used. Ozone, an invisible gas, is not emitted directly into the air, but forms when nitrogen oxides from fuel combustion and volatile organic gases from evaporated petroleum products react in the presence of sunshine. Ozone levels are highest during the warm months when there is strong sunshine, high temperatures and an inversion layer.

Nitrogen oxides are produced when fossil fuels are burned in motor vehicles, power plants, furnaces and turbines. Carbon monoxide is a by-product of combustion that comes almost entirely from motor vehicles. Fine particulates, which are emitted directly as smoke and diesel soot and form in the air out of nitrogen oxides and sulfur oxides, obscure visibility and can be inhaled deep into the lungs.

Historic Air Pollution Disasters

There have been several episodes in history which illustrate the harmful effects of acute short-term exposure to air pollution. They include:

Belgium's Meuse Valley

During a five-day fog in December 1930, 63 people died, most of the deaths occurring on the fourth and fifth days. Older persons with previously known diseases of the heart or lungs accounted for the majority of fatalities. The signs and symptoms were primarily those caused by a respiratory irritant. They include chest pain, cough, shortness of breath and irritation of the eyes. Sulfur dioxide gas is suspected as the cause of the disaster.

London, England

Three episodes during which heavy fogs and air pollution were associated, resulted in the death of nearly 5,000 people—in 1948, 1952, and 1956. The episode in December of 1952 alone, resulted in at least 3,000 deaths more than expected for that time of year. Although the increase was present in every age group, the greatest increase was in the age group of 45 years and over. More than 80% of these deaths occurred among individuals with known heart and respiratory disease.

During each of these incidents, comparable conditions were present: limited air supplies as a result of low-lying temperature inversions and faint winds, and a continuing heavy output of air pollution from multiple sources. Also, in none of the incidents was technology sophisticated enough to properly monitor the air and diagnosis of the specific causes of the illness and deaths were based on limited evidence gathered after the disasters.

(restore) what has already been lost.

Unfortunately, heavy timber cutting in tropical and temperate forests, overhunting, and overfishing are destroying renewable resources at a rapid rate and, in the process, undercutting the resource base upon which the future of humanity depends. From the viewpoint of long-term sustainability, the destruction of these resources is far more dangerous than the quick depletion of nonrenewable resources—oil and minerals—now under way.

Another key determinant of carrying capacity is the ability of the environment to assimilate and degrade waste. In ecosystems, waste is "handled" by dilution, decomposition, and recycling. Although these natural mechanisms have been adequate throughout most of human history, the advent of industrialization and rapid population growth over the past 100 years have begun to overwhelm them. Today, for example, many nutrient cycles have been overpowered by variety of products that support our way of life. The global carbon cycle, which has for centuries ensured a constant concentration of atmospheric carbon dioxide through the interactions of plants and animals, is one of the best examples of a natural system thrown out of balance by human activity. Nitrate and phosphate pollution in our oceans, lakes, and rivers, which result in algal blooms, also show how the sheer volume of waste from human activity can overwhelm nature.

The advent of synthetic chemicals, moreover, has also sabotaged nature's innate mechanism of waste control. Since naturally occurring bacteria do not contain the enzymes needed to decompose many of these molecules, synthetic chemicals often persist in the environment. They may hang around for decades, entering food chains and poisoning a wide range of species, or, as in the case of plastic, may persist for centuries, providing a perpetual reminder of human carelessness.

On all three counts—food, resources, and pollution—the Earth's carrying capacity is stretched thin and in places ripping. Living sustainably means learning to live within limits.

Why Have We Failed?

In the past two decades, governments the world over have generated a blizzard of rules and regulations to protect the environment. Private industries—some under duress, some on their own accord—have taken many initiatives to reduce pollution and use resources more efficiently. Tens of billions of dollars are spent each year on environmental protection by governments and private interests.

Unfortunately, most of the policies and actions that have resulted from this steady outpouring of legislative mandate and private initiative are fundamentally flawed. This is not to say that environmental protection efforts have been ineffective. Surely without them the condition of the environment would be much worse than it is today. My contention, however, is that many of our efforts are really nothing more than stopgap measures. Consider a few examples that point out the flaws in the environmental response.

Smokestack scrubbers have been a major element in pollution control. Installed on power plants, they reduce sulfur dioxide emissions, helping to decrease acid deposition. Unfortunately, scrubbers generate a highly toxic ash, which is typically dumped in landfills where it may leach into ground water. Scrubbers are symptomatic of an end-of-pipe control strategy that merely shifts pollutants from one medium to another and has resulted in nothing more than an elaborate and costly toxic shell game.

In other cases, pollution control efforts mandated by legislative bodies have been too narrowly focused. Catalytic converters in automobiles, for example, have been added to reduce carbon monoxide and hydrocarbons in exhaust gases. But the catalytic converters in use today do nothing to reduce carbon dioxide emissions, a major contributor to global warming. Nor do they limit nitrogen oxides, a component of photochemical smog, which plagues most cities, and acid rain. Catalytic converters are successful in what they do, but they don't go far enough.

Box 3.6. CARS AND THE ATMOSPHERE

Each time you burn 1 quart of gasoline, you are creating about 4.5 pounds of carbon dioxide, adding to the 22 billion tons of carbon dioxide that humans produce each year by burning fossil fuels.

An average air-conditioned automobile contains between 4.5 and 5.5 pounds of chlorofluorocarbon (CFC) coolant, which is the equivalent of about six refrigerators. About one pound of CFCs leak out of each car annually from vibration, whether the air-conditioning is in use or not.

Bits of airborne lead, cadmium, and asbestos are constantly emitted by automobiles due to the wear of tires, brakes, and clutch linings. These metals and minerals collect on roads and the landscape that surrounds them. The heavy metals are toxic to human beings.

Source : Environment 1995 version. Peter Raven, Linda Berg and George Johnson.

Finally, many improvements achieved by pollution control efforts are being offset by increases in population and consumption. Expensive sewage treatment plants, for instance, have helped to reduce pollution entering many rivers and streams in the United States, but increases in human population have resulted in an offsetting increase in nonpoint pollution—chemicals from lawns, streets, and so on—that frequently negate gains from sewage treatment plants.

The important point is that in most cases, environmental policy in the United States and elsewhere has been crafted to reduce environmental pollution and destruction, not to end the erosion of our life support system. That is to say, environmental policy was designed to clean up the mess a little, not to ensure a sustainable way of living and doing business on the planet. Policymakers have given little thought to the long-term sustainability of human activities.

If environmental policy is flawed, then it is because the wrong questions were asked early on. Instead of "How can we reduce pollution or environmental destruction?" a more appropriate question might have been "What do we need to do to live sustainably on the planet?" As you shall see, this is a fundamentally different question that leads to fundamentally different strategies.

Besides ignoring the question of sustainability, the environmental response the world over has focused on the symptoms of the crisis, such as air pollution, hazardous waste, and deforestation, while overlooking the root causes. This approach to environmental protection is not unlike that of a physician who prescribes nitroglycerine for a patient suffering chest pains but who fails to address the issue of lifestyle changes—a better diet, a reduction of stress, an active exercise program, and so on.

Today, more than ever, environmental policy requires strategies that address the underlying causes of the crisis. Anything else is inadequate.

At least six factors lie at the root of the sustainability dilemma. *First* and foremost is overpopulation, a problem to which I have already alluded. It can be summed up as too many people reproducing too quickly.

The *second* root cause is excessive resource consumption Over-consumption is particularly evident in the industrial world, and especially in North America, where energy, timber, food, water and a host of other resources are consumed in a mad frenzy to support an economy predicated on rapid throughput—that is, excessive production and consumption.

The *third* root cause is linearity. In most countries, resources follow a straight line from mines to manufacturing plants to consumers to landfills. Enormous amounts of waste are generated along the way and at the end of the line, and very little of it is recycled.

The *fourth* root cause is our addiction to fossil fuels. A host of environmental problems, including urban air pollution, global warming, acid deposition, oil pollution, and habitat destruction, stem from our heavy dependence on coal, oil, and natural gas. Few can deny that fact.

The *fifth* cause is inefficiency. Although there are encouraging improvements, most of us waste extraordinary amounts of energy, water, and other resources.

The *sixth* and final root cause of environmental deterioration is our values. Most industrial countries are driven by a frontier mentality. With its view of the earth as an unlimited supply of resources for human use, the frontier mentality places humans apart from nature and suggests that we are immune to natural laws. It also asserts that success stems from efforts to dominate or control nature. A growing body of evidence argues otherwise.

Steering a sustainable course will require systemic changes that confront the underlying causes of the environmental crisis head on. Ironically, the best advice in this area comes not from political science but from biology, where studies of undisturbed ecosystems yield simple yet timely advice to those of us who will step back from the din of modern life and listen.

The lessons we can learn from nature comprise the biological principles of sustainability These principles explain why undisturbed ecosystems persist in the absence of human intervention or in the absence of major geological change, and they offer a ray of hope in a world being ravaged by the frontier ways.

Applying biological principles to human civilization may seem outlandish. It is not. In fact, it may be our only hope of weaving the human economy and the human way of life back into the economy of nature and ensuring our survival in the long run. Applying these principles to ethics, government, industry and our own lives can help us end the destruction and heal the massive damage already wrought in the name of progress.

In Search of Instructions

Buckminster Fuller likened the earth to a giant spaceship. Equipped with intricate recycling mechanisms that provide its inhabitants with a continuous supply of nutrients, this celestial ball of rock, ice, and water is home to at least three million species, although the number is probably more likely 30 to 50 million.

Over a brief time span, one species, *Homo sapiens,* has become the dominant life force of the Earth. Standing on the brink of disaster, we ask ourselves, what it is we need to do.

Clearly, we don't need an operator's manual, a set of engineering instructions that tells us how to manage the earth; we need a co-operator's manual that teaches us how to fit into the cycles of nature's economy. Applying eco-logic to human endeavor, the co-operator's manual will teach us to live within the limits of the earth's carrying capacity.

It has been said that people and nations behave wisely once they have exhausted all other alternatives. Many believe that the time for wisdom is at hand. If we are smart, we will follow the logic and laws of nature and remake our world according to its patterns, which have proven successful throughout evolutionary history. The earth's wisdom is irrefutable. And, as a student of mine recently reminded me, nature is the master of sustainability.

....

Ecological Literacy

David W. Orr

*Education is the instruction of the intellect in the laws of
Nature*

— Thomas Henry Huxley

The crisis of sustainability, the fit between humanity and its habitat, is manifest in varying ways and degrees everywhere on earth. It is not only a permanent feature on the public agenda, for all practical purposes, it is the agenda. No other issue of politics, economics, and public policy will remain unaffected by the crisis of resources, population, climate change, species extinction, acid rain, deforestation, ozone depletion, and soil loss. Sustainability is about the terms and conditions of human survival, and yet we still educate at all levels as if no such crisis existed. The content of our curriculum and the process of education, with a few notable exceptions, has not changed. We have added computers to the scene, but mostly to do things we did before only faster. What is apparent, however, is that we do not worry about what our children and young people learn and how well they learn it until a crisis happens along. We have not yet begun to worry whether or not our children will know how to protect the biological resources upon which any economy ultimately depends.

The crisis cannot be solved by the same kind of education that helped create the problems. Against the test of sustainability, our ideas, theories, sciences, humanities, social sciences, pedagogy, and educational institutions have not measured up. Schools, colleges, and universities are part of the problem. What passes for environmental education is still mostly regarded as a frill to be cut when budgets get tight. Environmental education is done by teachers and faculty mostly on release time or on their own as an overload. Environmental concerns and the issues raised by the challenge of sustainability are still blithely ignored in the mainstream of nearly all the disciplines represented in the catalogs of our proudest institutions. From a casual sampling of the various professional journals, one would have little idea that humanity had any problems beyond methodological esoterica.

What is ecological literacy?

Literacy is the ability to read. Numeracy is the ability to count. Ecological literacy, according to Garrett Hardin, is the ability to ask "What then?" Considerable attention is properly being given to our shortcomings in teaching the young to read, count, and compute, but not nearly enough to ecological literacy. Reading, after all, is an ancient skill. And for most of the twentieth century we have been busy adding, subtracting, multiplying, dividing and now computing. But "what then?" questions have not come easy for us despite all of our formidable advances in other areas. Economists, who are certainly both numerate and numerous, have not asked the question often enough. Asking "What then?" on the west side of the Niemen River, or at Fort Laramie, would have saved a lot of trouble. For the same reason, "What then?" is also an appropriate question to ask before the last rain forests disappear, before the growth economy consumes itself into oblivion, and before we have warmed the planet intolerably.

The failure to develop ecological literacy is a sin of omission and of commission. Not only are we failing to teach the basics about the earth and how it works, but we are in fact teaching a large amount of stuff that is simply wrong. By failing to include ecological perspectives in any number of subjects, students are taught that ecology is unimportant for history, politics, economics, society, and so forth. And through television they learn that the earth is theirs for the taking. The result is a generation of ecological yahoos without a clue why the color of the water in their rivers is related to their food supply or why storms are becoming more severe as the planet warms. The same persons as adults will create businesses, vote, have families, and above all, consume. If they come to reflect on the discrepancy between the splendor of their private lives in a hotter, more toxic and violent world, as ecological illiterates they will have roughly the same success as one trying to balance a checkbook without knowing arithmetic.

Formation of attitudes

To become ecologically literate one must certainly be able to read and, I think, even like to read. Ecological literacy also presumes an ability to use numbers, and the ability to know what is countable and what is not, which is to say the limits of numbers. But these are indoor skills. Ecological literacy also requires the more demanding capacity to observe nature with insight, a merger of landscape and mindscape. "The interior landscape," in Barry Lopez's words, "responds to the character and subtlety of an exterior landscape; the shape of the individual mind is affected by land as it is by genes." The quality of thought is related to the ability to relate to "where on this earth one goes, what one touches, the patterns one observes in nature—the intricate history of one's life in the land, even a life in the city, where wind, the chirp of birds the line of a falling leaf, are known." The fact that this kind of intimate knowledge of our landscapes is rapidly disappearing can only impoverish our mental landscapes as well. People who do not know the ground on which they stand miss one of the elements of good thinking which is the capacity to distinguish between health and disease in natural systems and their relation to health and disease in human ones.

If literacy is driven by the search for knowledge, ecological literacy is driven by the sense of wonder, the sheer delight in being alive in a beautiful, mysterious, bountiful world. The darkness and disorder that we have brought to that world give ecological literacy an urgency it lacked a century ago. We can now look over the abyss and see the end of it all. Ecological literacy begins in childhood. To keep alive his inborn sense of wonder, a child, in Rachel Carson's words, needs the companionship of at least one adult who can share it, rediscovering with him the joy, excitement and mystery of the world we live in. The sense of wonder is rooted in the emotions or what F.O. Wilson has called "biophilia," which is simply the affinity for the living world. The nourishment of that affinity is the beginning point for the sense of kinship with life, without which literacy of any sort will not help much. This is to say that even a thorough knowledge of the facts of life and of the threats to it, will not save us in the absence of the feeling of kinship with life of the sort that cannot entirely be put into words.

There are, I think, several reasons why ecological literacy has been so difficult for Western culture. *First,* it implies the ability to think broadly, to know something of what is hitched to what. This ability is being lost in an age of specialization. Scientists of the quality of Rachel Carson or Aldo Leopold are rarities who must buck the pressures towards narrowness and also endure a great deal of professional rejection and hostility. By inquiring into the relationship between chlorinated hydrocarbon pesticides and bird populations, Rachel Carson was asking an ecological question. Many others failed to ask, not because they did not like birds, but because they had not, for whatever reasons, thought beyond the conventional categories. To do so would have required that they relate their food system to the decline in the number of birds in their neighborhood. This means that they would have had some direct knowledge of farms and farming practices, as well as a comprehension of ornithology. To think in ecological manner presumes a breadth of experience with healthy natural systems, both of which are increasingly rare. It also presumes that the persons be willing and able to "think at right angles" to their particular specialization's, as Leopold put it.

Ecological literacy is difficult, *second,* because we have come to believe that education is solely an indoor activity. A good part of it, of necessity, must be, but there is a price. William Morton Wheeler once compared the naturalist with the professional biologist in these words: "The naturalist is primarily an observer and fond of outdoor life, a collector, a classifier, a describer, deeply impressed by the overwhelming intricacy of natural phenomena and reveling in their very complexity." The biologist, on the other hand, "is oriented toward and dominated by ideas, and rather terrified or oppressed by the intricate hurly-burly of concrete sensuous reality...he is a denizen of the laboratory. His besetting sin is oversimplification and the tendency to undue isolation of the organisms he studies from their natural environment." Since Wheeler wrote, ecology has become increasingly specialized and, one suspects, remote from its subject matters. Ecology, like most learning worthy of the effort, is an applied subject. Its goal is not just a comprehension of how the world works, but in the light of the knowledge, a life lived accordingly.

The decline in the capacity for aesthetic appreciation is a *third* factor working against ecological literacy. We have become comfortable with all kinds of ugliness and seem incapable of effective protest against its purveyors: urban developers, busi- nessmen, government officials, television executives, timber and mining companies, utilities, and advertisers. Rene Dubos once stated that our greatest disservice to our children was to give them the belief that ugliness was somehow normal. But disordered landscapes are not just an aesthetic problem. Ugliness signifies a more fundamental disharmony between people and between people and the land. Ugliness is, I think, the surest sign of disease, or what is now being called "unsustainability." Show me the hamburger stands, neon ticky-tacky strips leading toward every city in America, and the shopping malls, and I'll show you devastated rain forests, a decaying countryside, a politically dependent population, and toxic waste dumps. It is all of a fabric.

And this is the heart of the matter: To see things in their wholeness is politically threatening. To understand that our manner of living, so comfortable for some, is linked to cancer rates in migrant laborers in California, the disappearance of tropical rain forests, fifty thousand toxic dumps across the U.S.A., and the depletion of the ozone layer, is to see the need for a change in our way of life. To see things whole is to see both the wounds we have inflicted on the natural world in the name of mastery and those we have inflicted on ourselves and on our children for no good reason, whatever our stated intentions. Real ecological literacy is radicalizing in that it forces us to reckon with the roots of our ailments, not just with their symptoms. For this reason, I think it leads to revitalization and broadening of the concept of citizenship to include membership in a planetwide community of humans and living things.

Ecological literacy is becoming more difficult, I believe, not because there are fewer books about nature, but because there is less opportunity for the direct experience of it. Fewer people grow up on farms or in rural areas where access is easy and where it is easy to learn a degree of competence and self-confidence toward the natural world. Where the ratio between the human-created environment to the purely natural world exceeds some point, the sense of place can only be a sense of habitat. One finds the habitat familiar and/or likeable but without any real sense of belonging in the natural world. A sense of place requires more direct contact with the natural aspects of a place, with soils, landscape, and wildlife. The sense is lost as we move down the continuum towards the totaled urban environment where nature exists in tiny, isolated fragments by permission only. Said differently, this is an argument for more urban parks, summer camps, green belts, wilderness areas, and public seashores. If we must live in an increasingly urban world, let's make it one of well-designed compact green cities that include trees, river parks, meandering greenbelts, and urban farms where people can see, touch, and experience nature in a variety of ways. In fact, no other cities will be sustainable in a greenhouse world.

Ecological literacy and formal education

The goal of ecological literacy as I have described it, has striking implications for that part of education that must occur in classrooms, libraries, and laboratories: To the extent that most educators have noticed the environment, they have regarded it as a set of problems which are: (1) solvable (unlike dilemmas, which are not) by (2) the analytic tools and methods of reductionist science which (3) create value-neutral, technological remedies that will not create even worse side effects. Solutions, therefore, originate at the top of society, from governments and corporations, and are passed down to a passive citizenry in the form of laws, policies, and technologies. The results, it is assumed, will be socially, ethically, politically, and humanly desirable and the will to live and to sustain a humane culture can be preserved in a technocratic society. In other words, business can go on as usual. Since there is not particular need for an ecologically literate and ecologically competent public, environmental education is most often regarded as an extra in the curriculum, not as a core requirement or as an aspect pervading the entire educational process.

Clearly, some parts of the crisis can be accurately described as problems. Some of these can be solved by technology, particularly those that require increased resource efficiency. It is a mistake, however, to think that all we need is better technology, not an ecologically literate and caring public willing to help reduce the scale of problems by reducing its demands on the environment and to accept (even demand) public policies that require sacrifices. It all comes down to whether the public understands the relation between its well-being and the health of the natural systems.

For this to occur, we must rethink both the substance and the process of education at all levels. What does it mean to educate people to live sustainably, going, in Aldo Leopold's words, from "conqueror of the land community to plain member and citizen of it?" However it is applied in practice, the answer will rest on six foundations.

The *first* is the recognition that all education is environmental education. By what is included or excluded, emphasized or ignored, students learn that they are a part of or apart from the natural world. Through all education we inculcate the ideas of careful stewardship or carelessness. Conventional education, by and large, has been a celebration of all that is human to the exclusion of our dependence on nature. As a result, students frequently resemble what Wendell Berry has called "itinerant professional vandals", persons devoid of any sense of place or stewardship, or inkling of why these are important.

Second, environmental issues are complex and cannot be understood through a single discipline or department. Despite a decade or more of discussion and experimentation, interdisciplinary education remains an unfulfilled promise. The failure occurred, I submit, because it was tried within discipline-centric institutions. A more promising approach is to reshape institutions to function as transdisciplinary laboratories that include components such as agriculture, solar technologies, forestry, land management, wildlife, waste cycling, architectural design, and economics. Part of the task, then, of Earth-centered education is the study of interactions across the boundaries of conventional knowledge and experience.

Third, for inhabitants, education occurs in part as a dialogue with a place and has the characteristics of good conversation. Formal education happens mostly as a monologue of human interest, desires, and accomplishments that drowns out all other sounds. It is the logical outcome of the belief that we are alone in a dead world of inanimate matter, energy flows, and biogeochemical cycles. But true conversation can occur only if we acknowledge the existence and interests of the other. In conversation, we define ourselves, but in relation to another. The quality of conversation does not rest on the brilliance of one or the other person. It is more like a dance in which the artistry is mutual.

In good conversation, words represent reality faithfully. And words have power. They can enliven or deaden, elevate or degrade, but they are never neutral, because they affect our perception and ultimately our behavior. The use of words such as "resources," "manage," "channelize," "engineer," and "produce" makes our relation to nature a monologue rather than a conversation. The language of nature includes the sounds of animals, whales, birds, insects, wind, and water–a language more ancient and basic than human speech. Its books are the etchings of life on the face of the land. To hear this language requires a patient, disciplined study of the natural world. But it is a language for which we have an affinity.

Fourth, it follows that the way education occurs is as important as its content. Students taught environmental awareness in a setting that does not alter their relationship to basic life-support systems learn that it is sufficient to intellectualize, emote, or posture about such things without having to live differently. Environmental education ought to change the way people live, not just how they talk. This understanding of education is drawn from the writings of John Dewey, Alfred North Whitehead, J. Glenn Gray, Paulo Friere, Ivan Illich, and Eliot Wigginton. Learning in this view best occurs in response to real needs and the life situation of the learner. The radical distinctions typically drawn between teacher and student, between the school and the community, and those between areas of knowledge, are dissolved. Real learning is participatory and experimental, not just didactic. The flow can be two ways—between teachers, who best function as facilitators, and students who are expected to be active agents in defining what is learned and how.

Fifth, experience in the natural world is both an essential part of understanding the environment, and conducive to good thinking. Experience, properly conceived, trains the intellect to observe the land carefully and to distinguish between health and its opposite. Direct experience is an antidote to indoor, abstract learning. It is also a wellspring of good thinking. Understanding nature demands a disciplined and observant intellect.

Sixth, education relevant to the challenge of building a sustainable society will enhance the learner's competence with natural systems. For reasons once explained by Whitehead and Dewey, practical competence is an indispensable source of good thinking. Good thinking proceeds from the friction between reflective thought and real problem. Aside from its effects on thinking, practical competence will be essential if sustainability requires, as I think it does, that people must take an active part in rebuilding their homes, businesses, neighborhoods, communities, and towns. Shortening supply lines for food, energy, water, and materials–while recycling waste locally–implies a high degree of competence not necessary in a society dependent on central vendors and experts.

The aim of ecological literacy

If these can be taken as the foundations of Earth-centered education, what can be said of its larger purpose? In a phrase, it is that quality of mind that seeks out connections. It is the opposite of the specialization and narrowness, characteristic of most education. The ecologically literate person has the knowledge necessary to comprehend interrelatedness, and an attitude of care or stewardship.

Ecological literacy, further, implies a broad understanding of how people and societies relate to each other and to natural systems, and how they might do so sustainably. It presumes both an awareness of the interrelatedness of life and knowledge of how the world works as a physical system. To ask, let alone answer, "What then?" questions presumes an understanding of concepts such as carrying capacity, overshoot, Liebig's Law of the minimum, thermodynamics, trophic levels, energetic, and succession. Ecological literacy presumes that we understand our place in the story of evolution. It is to know that our health, well-being and ultimately our survival depend on working with, not against, natural forces. The basis for ecological literacy, then, is the comprehension of the inter-relatedness of life grounded in the study of natural history, ecology, and thermodynamics. It is to understand that: "There ain't no such thing as a free lunch." "You can never throw anything away"; and "The first law of intelligent tinkering is to keep all of the pieces." It is also to understand, with Leopold, that we live in a world of wounds senselessly inflicted on nature and on ourselves.

A second stage in ecological literacy is to know something of the speed of the crisis that is upon us. It is to know magnitudes, rates, and trends of population growth, species extinction, soil loss, deforestation, desertification, climate change, ozone depletion, resource exhaustion, air and water pollution, toxic and radioactive contamination, resource and energy use—in short, the vital signs of the planet and its ecosystems. Becoming ecologically literate is to understand the human enterprise for what it is a sudden eruption in the enormity of evolutionary time.

Ecological literacy requires a comprehension of the dynamics of the modern world. The best starting place is to read the original rationale for the domination of nature found in the writings of Bacon, Descartes, and Galileo. Here one finds the justification for the union of science with power and the case for separating ourselves from nature in order to control it more fully. To comprehend the idea of controlling nature, one must fathom the sources of the urge to power and the paradox of rational means harnessed to insane ends portrayed in Marlowe's "Doctor Faustus", Mary Shelley's "Frankenstein", Melville's "Moby-Dick", and Dostoevsky's "Legend of the Grand Inquisitor."

Ecological literacy, then, requires a thorough understanding of the ways in which people and whole societies have become destructive. The ecologically literate person will appreciate something of how social structures, religion, science, politics, technology, patriarchy, culture, agriculture, and human cussedness combine as causes of our predicament.

The diagnosis of the causes of our plight is only half of the issue. But before we can address solutions there are several issues that demand clarification. "Nature," for example, is variously portrayed as "red in tooth and claw," or like the film "Bambi," full of sweet little critters. Economists see nature as natural resources to be used; the backpacker as a wellspring of transcendent values. We are no longer clear about our own nature, whether we are made in the image of God, or are merely a machine or computer, or animal. These are not trivial, academic issues. Unless we can make reasonable distinctions between what is natural and what is not, and why that difference is important, we are liable to be at the mercy of the engineers who want to remake all of nature, including our own.

Environmental literacy also requires a broad familiarity with the development of ecological consciousness. The best history of the concept of ecology is Donald Worster's "Nature's Economy." It is unclear whether the science of ecology will be the last of the old sciences, or the first of the new. As the former, ecology is the science of efficient resource management. As the first of the new sciences, ecology is the basis for a broader search for pattern and meaning. As such it cannot avoid issues of values, and the ethical questions raised most succinctly in Leopold's "The Land Ethic."

The study of environmental problems is an exercise in despair unless it is regarded as only a preface to the study, design, and implementation of solutions. The concept of sustainability implies a radical change in the institutions and patterns that we have come to accept as normal. It begins with ecology as the basis for the redesigns of technology, cities, farms and educational institutions, and with a change in metaphors from mechanical to organic, industrial to biological. As part of the change we will need alternative measures of well-being such as those proposed by Amory Lovin (least-cost end-use analysis), H.T. Odum (energy accounting) and John Cobb (index of sustainable welfare). Sustainability also implies a different approach to technology, one that gives greater priority to those that are smaller in scale, less environmentally destructive, and rely on the free services of natural systems. Not infrequently, technologies with this characteristic are also highly cost-effective, especially when subsidies for competing technologies are leveled out.

If sustainability represents a minority tradition, it is nonetheless a long one dating back at least to Jefferson. Students should not be considered ecologically literate until they have read Thoreau, Kropotkin, Muir, Albert Howard, Alfred North Whitehead, Gandhi, Schweitzer, Aldo Leopold, Lewis Mumford, Rachel Carson, E.F. Schumacher, and Wendell Berry.

There are alternatives to the present patterns that have remained dormant or isolated, not because they did not work, were poorly thought out, or were impractical, but because they were not tried. In contrast to the directions of modern society, this tradition emphasizes democratic participation, the extension of ethical obligations to the land community, careful ecological design, simplicity, widespread competence with natural systems, the sense of place, holism, decentralization, and human-scaled technologies and communities. It is a tradition grounded in the belief that life is sacred and not to be carelessly expended on the ephemeral. It is a tradition that challenges militarism, injustice, ecological destruction, and authoritarianism, while supporting all of those actions that lead to real peace, fairness, sustainability, and people's right to participate in those decisions that affect their lives. Ultimately, it is a tradition built on a view of ourselves as finite and fallible creatures living in a world limited by natural laws. The contrasting Promethean view, given force by the success of technology, holds that we should remove all limits, whether imposed by nature, human nature, or morality. Its slogan is found emblazoned on the advertisements of the age. "You can have it all" (Michelob Beer), or "Your world should know no limits" (Merrill Lynch). The ecologically literate citizen will recognize these immediately for what they are: the stuff of epitaphs. Ecological literacy leads in other, and more durable directions towards prudence, stewardship and the celebration of the Creation.

••••

WHEN EARTH'S LAST PICTURE IS PAINTED

When Earth's last picture is painted and the tubes are
    Twisted and dried,
When the oldest colors have faded, and the youngest
    critic has died,
We shall rest, and, faith, we shall need it—lie down for an
    Aeon or two,
Till the Master of All Good Workmen shall put us to work
    anew.

And those that were good shall be happy : they shall sit in
    a golden chair;
They shall splash at a ten-league canvas with brushes of
    comets' hair.
They shall find real saints to draw from—Magdalene,
    Peter, and Paul;
They shall work for an age at a sitting and never be tired
    at all!

And only The Master shall praise us, and only The Master
    Shall blame;
And no one shall work for money, and no one shall work
    For fame,
But each for the joy of the working, and each, in his
    Separate star,
Shall draw the Thing as he sees It for the God of things as
    They are!

                                    L'Evnoi to `The Seven Seas'
                                    — Rudyard Kipling

Human ignorance and Ecological Doom

" And suddenly, one more impatient cried – who is the potter, pray and who the Pot ? "

— *Omar Khayyam*

A SOUND OF THUNDER

Ray Bradbury

*With the realization of the importance of even our
smallest acts, we may come to perceive our tremendous
impact upon our environment — the only
world we have.*

The sign on the wall seemed to quaver under a film of sliding warm water. Eckels felt his eyelids blink out his stare, and the sign burned in this momentary darkness:

> TIME SAFARI, INC.
> SAFARIS TO ANY YEAR IN THE PAST.
> YOU NAME THE ANIMAL.
> WE TAKE YOU THERE.
> YOU SHOOT IT.

"Does this safari guarantee I come back alive?"

"We guarantee nothing," said the official, "except the dinosaurs." He turned. "This is Mr. Travis, your Safari Guide in the Past. He'll tell you what and where to shoot. If he says no shooting, no shooting. If you disobey instructions, there's a stiff penalty of another ten thousand dollars, plus possible government action, on your return."

Eckels remembered the wording in the advertisements to the letter. 'Out of chars and ashes, out of dust and coals, like golden salamanders, the old years, the green years, might leap; roses sweeten the air, white hair turn Iris-black, wrinkles vanish; all, everything fly back to seed, flee death, rush down to their beginnings, suns rise in western skies and set in glorious east, moons eat themselves opposite to the custom, all and everything cupping one in another like Chinese boxes, rabbits into hats, all and everything returning to the fresh death, the seed death, the green death, to the time before the beginning. A touch of a hand might do it, the merest touch of a hand.'

"Unbelievable." Eckels breathed, the light of the Machine on his thin face. "A real Time Machine." He shook his head. "Makes you think. If the election had gone badly yesterday, I might be here now running away from the results. Thanks God Keith won. He'll make a fine President of the United States."

"Yes," said the man behind the desk. "We're lucky. If Deutscher had gotten in, we'd have the worst kind of dictatorship. There's an anti-everything man for you, a militarist, anti-Christ, anti-human, anti-intellectual. People called us up, you know, joking but not joking. Said if Deutscher became President they wanted to go live in 1492. Of course it's not our business to conduct escapes, but to form safaris. Anyway, Keith's President now. All you got to worry about is-"

"Shooting my dinosaur," Eckels finished it for him.

"A Tyrannosaurus rex. The Tyrant Lizard, the most incredible monster in history. Sign this release. Anything happens to you, we are not responsible. Those dinosaurs are hungry."

"Good luck," said the man behind the desk. "Mr. Travis, he is all yours."

They moved silently across the room, taking their guns with them, toward the Machine, toward the silver metal and the roaring light.

First a day and then a night and then a day and then a night, then it was day-night-day-night-day. A week, a month, a year, a decade! A.D. 2055. A.D. 2019. 1999! 1957! Gone! The Machine roared.

There were four other men in the Machine. Travis, the Safari Leader, his assistant, Lesperance, and two other hunters, Billings and Kramer. They sat looking at each other, and the years blazed around them.

The Machine howled. Time was a film run backward. Suns fled and ten million moons fled after them. "Think," said Eckels. "Every hunter that ever lived would envy us today. This makes Africa seem like Illinois."

The Machine slowed; its scream fell to a murmur. The Machine stopped.

The sun stopped in the sky.

"Christ is not born yet," said Travis. "Moses has not gone to the mountain to talk with God. The Pyramids are still in the earth, waiting to be cut out and put up. *Remember* that. Alexander, Caesar, Napoleon, Hitler — none of them exist."

The man nodded.

"That" — Mr. Travis pointed — "is the jungle of sixty million, two thousand and fifty-five years before President Keith."

He indicated a metal path that struck off into green wilderness, over streaming swamp, among giant ferns and palms.

"And that," he said, "is the Path?, laid by Time Safari for your use. It floats six inches above the earth. Doesn't touch so much as one grass blade, flower or tree. It is an anti-gravity metal. Its purpose is to keep you from touching this world of the past in any way. Stay on the Path. Don't go off it. I repeat, *don't go off.* For *any* reason! If you fall off, there's a penalty. And don't shoot any animal we don't okay."

"Why?" asked Eckels.

"We don't want to change the Future. We don't belong here in the Past. The government does not *like* us here. We have to pay big graft to keep our franchise. A Time Machine is finicky business. Not knowing it, we might kill an important animal, a small bird, a roach, a flower even, thus destroying an important link in a growing species."

"That's not clear," said Eckels.

"All right," Travis continued, "say we accidentally kill one mouse here. That means all the future families of this one particular mouse are destroyed, right?"

"Right."

"And all the families of the families of the families of that one mouse! With a stamp of your foot, you annihilate first one, then a dozen, then a thousand, a million, a *billion* possible mice!"

"So they are dead," said Eckels, "So what?"

"So what?" Travis snorted quietly. "Well, what about the foxes that'll need those mice to survive? For want of ten mice, a fox dies.

For want of ten foxes, a lion starves. For want of a lion, all manners of insects, vultures, infinite billions of life forms are thrown into chaos and destruction. Eventually it all boils down to this: fifty-nine million years later, a caveman, one of a dozen on the *entire world*, goes hunting wild boar or saber-toothed tiger for food. But you, friend, have *stepped* on all the tigers in that region. By stepping on *one* single mouse. So the caveman starves. And the caveman, please note, is not just *any* expendable man, no! He is an *entire future nation*. From his loins would have sprung ten sons. From *their* loins one hundred sons, and thus onward to a civilization. Destroy this one man, and you destroy a race, a people, an entire history of life. It is comparable to slaying some of Adam's grandchildren. The stomp of your foot on one mouse, could start an earthquake, the effects of which could shake our earth and destinies down through Time to their very foundations. So be careful. Stay on the Path. *Never* step off!"

"I see," said Eckels. "Then it would not pay for us even to touch the *grass?*"

"Correct. Crushing certain plants could add up infinitesimally. A little error here would multiply in sixty million years, all out of proportion. Of course may be our theory is wrong. May be Time *cannot* be changed by us. Or may be it can be changed only in little subtle ways. Who knows? Who really can say he knows? We don't know. We're guessing. But until we do know for certain whether our messing around in Time can make a big roar or a little rustle in history, we're being careful. This Machine, this Path, your clothing and bodies were sterilized, as you know, before the journey. We wear these oxygen helmets so we can't introduce our bacteria into an ancient atmosphere."

"How do we know which animals to shoot?"

"They're marked with red paint," said Travis. "Today, before our journey, we sent Lesperance here back with the Machine. He came to this particular era and followed certain animals."

"Studying them?"

"Right," said Lesperance, "I track them through their entire existence, noting which of them lives longest. Very few. How many times they mate. When I find one that's going to die when a tree falls on him, or one that drowns in a tar pit, I note the exact hour, minute, and second. I shoot a paint bomb. It leaves a red patch on his side. Then I correlate our arrival in the Past so that we meet the monster not more than two minutes before he would have died anyway. This way, we kill only animals with no future, that are never going to mate again. You see how *careful* we are?"

Eckels smiled palely.

They were ready to leave the Machine.

Sounds like music and sounds like flying tents filled the sky, and those were pterodactyls soaring with cavernous gray wings, gigantic bats of delirium and night fever.

Eckels flushed. "Where's our *Tyrannosaurus?*"

Lesperance checked his wristwatch. "Up ahead. We'll bisect his trail in sixty seconds. Look for the red paint! Don't shoot till we give the word. Stay on the Path, *Stay on the Path!*"

They moved forward in the wind of morning.

"Strange," murmured Eckels. "Up ahead, sixty million years, election Day over; Keith made President; Everyone celebrating. And here we are, a million years lost, and they don't exist. The things we worried about for months, a life-time, not even born or thought of yet."

"Safety catches off, everyone!" ordered Travis. "You, first shot, Eckels. Second, Billings. Third, Kramer."

A sound of thunder.

Out of the mist, one hundred yards away, came *Tyrannosaurus rex.*

"It," whispered Eckels. "It...."

"Sh!"

It came on great oiled, resilient, striding legs. It towered thirty feet above half of the trees, a great evil god, folding its delicate watchmaker's claws close to its oily reptilian chest. Each lower leg was a piston, a thousand pounds of white bone, sunk in thick ropes of muscle, sheathed over in a gleam of pebbled skin. Each thigh was a ton of meat, ivory and steel mesh. And from the great breathing cage of the upper body those two delicate arms dangled out front, arms with hands which might pick up and examine men like toys, while the snake neck coiled. And the head itself, a ton of sculptured stone, lifted easily upon the sky. Its mouth gaped, exposing a fence of teeth like daggers. Its eyes rolled, ostrich eggs, empty of all expression save hunger.

"It can't be killed." Eckels pronounced this verdict quietly, as if there could be no argument. He had weighed the evidence and this was his considered opinion. The rifle in his hands seemed a cap gun. "We were fools to come. This is impossible."

"Shut up!" hissed Travis.

"Nightmare."

"Turn around," commanded Travis. "Walk quietly to the Machine. We'll remit one half your fee."

"There's the red paint on its chest!"

The Tyrant Lizard raised itself. Its armored flesh glittered like a thousand green coins. The coins, crusted with slime, steamed. In the slime, tiny insects wriggled, so that the entire body seemed to twitch and undulate, even while the monster itself did not move. It exhaled. The stink of raw flesh blew down the wilderness.

Eckels seemed to be numb.

He took a few steps, blinking, shuffling.

"Not *that* way!"

Eckels, not looking back, walked blindly to the edge of the Path, his gun limp in his arms, stepped off the Path, and walked, not knowing it, in the jungle. His feet sank into green moss. His legs moved him, and he felt alone and remote from the events behind.

The rifles cracked again. The great level of the reptile's tail swung up, lashed sideways. Trees exploded in clouds of leaf and branch. The Monster twitched its jeweler's hands down to fondle at the men, to twist them in half, to crush them like berries, to cram them into its teeth and its screaming throat. Its boulder-stone eyes leveled with the men. They saw themselves mirrored. They fired at the metallic eyelids and the blazing black irises.

Like a stone idol, like a mountain avalanche, *Tyrannosaurus* fell. Thundering, it clutched trees, pulled them with it. It wrenched and tore the metal Path. The men flung themselves back and away. The body hit, ten tons of cold flesh and stone. The guns fired. The Monster lashed its armored tail, twitched its snake jaws and lay still. A fount of blood spurted from its throat. Somewhere inside, a sac of fluids burst. Sickening gushes drenched the hunters. They stood, red and glistening.

The thunder faded. The jungle was silent.

Billings and Kramer sat on the pathway and threw up. Travis and Lesperance stood with smoking rifles, cursing steadily.

In the Time Machine, on his face, Eckels lay shivering. He had found his way back to the Path, climbed into the Machine.

They wiped the blood from their helmets. They began to curse too. The Monster lay, a hill of solid flesh. Within, you could hear the sighs and murmurs as the furthest chambers of it died, the organs malfunctioning, liquids running a final instant from pocket to sac to spleen, everything shutting off, closing up forever. It was like standing by a wrecked locomotive.

Another cracking sound. Overhead, a gigantic tree branch broke from its heavy mooring, fell. It crashed upon the dead beast with finality.

"There." Lesperance checked his watch. "Right on time. That's the giant tree that was scheduled to fall and kill this animal originally." He glanced at the two hunters. "You want the trophy picture?"

"What?"

"We can't take a trophy back to the Future. The body has to stay right here where it would have died originally, so the insects, birds, and bacteria can get at it, as they were intended to. Everything in balance. The body stays.

The two men let themselves be led along the metal Path. They sank wearily into the Machine cushions.

A sound on the floor of the Time Machine stiffened them. Eckels
sat there, shivering.

"I'm sorry," he said at last.

"Get up!" cried Travis.

Eckels got up.

"Go out on that Path alone," said Travis. He had his rifle pointed.
"You're not coming back in the Machine. We're leaving you here!"

Lesperance seized Travis' arm. "Wait—"

"Stay out of this!" Travis shook his hand away. ?"This fool nearly
killed us. But it isn't *that* so much, no. It's his *shoes!* Look at them!
He ran off the Path. That *ruins* us! We'll forfeit! Thousands of dollars
of insurance! We guarantee no one leaves the Path. He left it. Oh,
the fool! I'll have to report to the government. They might revoke
our license to travel. Who knows *what* he's done to Time, to History!"

"Take it easy. All he did was kick up some dirt.'

"How do we *know?*' cried Travis. "We don't know anything!
It's all a mystery! Get out of here, Eckels!"

Eckels fumbled his shirt. "I'll pay anything. A hundred thousand
dollars!"

Travis glared at Eckels' checkbook and spat.

"The Monster's dead, you idiot. The bullets! The bullets can't
be left behind. They don't belong in the Past; they might change
anything. Here's my knife. Dig them out!"

The jungle was alive again, full of the old tremorings and bird cries.
Eckels turned slowly to regard the primeval garbage dump, that hill of
nightmares and terror.

He returned, shuddering, five minutes later, his arms soaked and
red to the elbows. He held out his hands. Each held a number of
steel bullets. Then he fell. He lay where he fell, not moving.

"Switch on. Let's go home."

1492. 1776. 1812.

They cleaned their hands and faces. They changed their caking shirts and pants. Eckels was up and around again, not speaking. Travis glared at him for a full ten minutes.

"Don't look at me," cried Eckels. "I haven't done anything."

"Who can tell?"

"Just ran off the Path, that's all, a little mud on my shoes - what do you want me to do, get down and pray?"

"We might need it. I'm warning you, Eckels, I might kill you yet. I've got my gun ready."

I'm innocent. I've done nothing!"

1999. 2000. 2055.

The Machine stopped.

"Get out," said Travis.

The room was there as they had left it. But not the same as they had left it. The same man sat behind the same desk.

Travis looked around swiftly. "Everything okay here?" he snapped.

"Fine. Welcome home!"

Travis did not relax. He seemed to be looking at the very atoms of the air itself, at the way the sun poured through the one high window.

"Okay, Eckels, get out. Don't ever come back."

Eckels could not move.

"You heard me," said Travis. "What're you *staring* at?"

Eckels stood smelling the air, and there was a thing to the air, a chemical taint so subtle, so slight, that only a faint cry of his subliminal senses warned him it was there. His flesh twitched. His hands twitched. He stood drinking the oddness with the pores of his body. Somewhere, someone must have been screaming one of those whistles that only a dog can hear. His body screamed silence in return. Beyond this room, beyond this wall, beyond this man who was not quite the same man seated at this desk that was not quite the same desk . . . lay an entire world of streets and people. What sort of world it was now, there was no telling. But the immediate thing was the sign painted on the office wall, the same sign he had read earlier today on first entering.

Somehow, the sign had changed:

TYME SEFARI INC.

SEFARIS TY ANY YEER EN THE PAST.

YU NAIM THE ANIMALL.

WEE TAKEYUTHAIR.

YU SHOOT ITT.

Eckels felt himself fall into a chair. He fumbled crazily at the thick slime on his boots. He held up a clod of dirt, trembling. "No, it *can't* be. Not a *little* thing like that. No!"

Embedded in the mud, glistening green and gold and black, was a butterfly, very beautiful and very dead.

"Not a little thing like *that!* Not a butterfly!" cried Eckels.

It fell to the floor, an exquisite thing, a small thing that could upset balances and knock down a line of small dominoes and then big dominoes and then gigantic dominoes, all down the years across Time. Eckels' mind whirled. It *couldn't* be important! Could it?

His face was cold. His mouth trembled, asking: "Who — who won the presidential election yesterday?"

The man behind the desk laughed. "You Joking?" You know very well. Deutscher, of course! Who else? Not that fool weakling Keith. We got an iron man now, a man with guts!" The official stopped. "What's wrong?"

Eckels moaned. He dropped to his knees. He scrabbled at the golden butterfly with shaking fingers. "Can't we," he pleaded to the world, to himself, to the officials, to the Machine, "can't we take it *back,* can't we *make* it alive again? Can't we start over? Can't we..."

He did not move. Eyes shut, he waited, shivering. He heard Travis breathe loud in the room; he heard Travis shift his rifle, click the safety catch and raise the weapon.

There was a sound of thunder.

••••

The Malthusian Ghost

Carlos Hernandez and Rashmi Mayur.

*The idea that population growth guarantees a better life –
financially or otherwise–is a myth that only those who sell
diapers, baby carriages and the like have any right to believe.*

– Fairfield Osborne

The Malthusian ghost is stalking the earth. Looking at the number
of humans inhabiting the world, nearly 6 billion, and their
uncontrolled increase, 80 million annually, it seems that the
human avalanche is covering the whole world. Almost 80% of
the people live in Africa, Asia and Latin America and 90% of the
growth is taking place there. If the inundation of the humans
continues at the present rate, the number will reach 10.5 billion
by around 2050 AD and it may stabilize at 11 billion sometimes
thereafter. This is frightening. The cruel fact of the world is that
there are too many people proliferating too fast for it to
accommodate. Many environmental scientists believe that the
earth's environment is already overstressed and its biological
systems are on the verge of breakdown. Our survival is
threatened.

But if you go around the world, particularly to those parts
of the world —Sub-Sahara Africa or India or Pakistan —where
enormous number of people are concentrated and living in
wretched poverty, you seldom get a feeling that the people and
their leaders know or understand the catastrophe of their
numbers, which are on a runaway path. By the time a day is over,
about 260,000 people are added to these poor countries with no
hope for their progeny. Africa, one of the poorest regions of the
world, has about 780 million people increasing at the annual
growth of 2.6% a year. By 2025, the region will have 1.5 billion
people, that is more than double the population of Europe. On

the other hand, Europe, one of the richest parts of the world, has 730 million people. Its numbers will decline below 700 million. The irony of this contrast is in the fact that while average per capita income of an African is less than $300 annually, it is $30,000 in Europe. Europeans are a high consuming society.

The largest population in the world inhabits Asia, with annual growth rate of 1.4%, thanks to the successful population control programs of China, with 1.2 billion people increasing at 1.6%. Asia's number is staggering. Almost 3 Australias are added in Asia every year. The situation is critical in South Asia — India, Bangladesh, Pakistan, Nepal, Sri Lanka — where, as in Africa, all the ecological, economic and social systems are disintegrating.

In the developing world, the region, which has made rapid progress in fertility control is Latin America and the Caribbean — mainly due to fast urbanization during the last 25 years. Almost 70% of the people live in cities and towns in this region, while in Asia and Africa, more than 70% live in rural and tribal areas. With 500 million people in this region increasing annually at 1.5%, it is a classic example of poverty, miseries and the environmental collapse due to unplanned and mindless industrialization.

The richest part of the world, the North America, has 305 million people increasing at the rate of 0.8% a year. The most prolific consumers of the planet inhabit the region.

If one examines the above profile of the earth in terms of the population distribution and consumption, the scenario of the world's human tragedy and the earth's ecological collapse become clear. For every American or European born, the total resource burden on the planet equals about 55 children born in Asia or Africa. Therefore, if our estimations are correct, then we are on a runaway course of multiplying human population and proliferating consumption. The consequences of this anomaly are evident in the global malignancy: By the dawn of the new millennium, almost 100,000 species of birds, animals and plants will have disappeared to make room for 150 million humans. By 2025, if the present imbalance continues, almost 50% of the remaining estimated 40 million species will become extinct.

We do recognize that the crisis of the technological age is rooted in the self-destructive consumerism. That does not diminish the fact that the human numbers have already crossed all the resource limits of the planet's capacity, almost twice over. There is another calamity in a world based on cruel inequities and that is the expansion of the increasing number of people living in sub human conditions of despondency.

The World Bank President, James Wolfensohn recently bemoaned that 1.3 billion people in the world were living in the state of desperation. The Food and Agriculture Organization laments that one out of six people in the world lives in perpetual state of hunger. The World Health Organization wails that almost fifty five thousand children succumb to malnutrition and preventable diseases every day. It should be emphasized here that all these tragedies occur in the developing world.

There is another phenomenon of this century which must be highlighted: urbanization. Almost 52% of the people in the world live in cities and towns. Some cities like Mexico city (21 million), Sao Paulo (18 million), Mumbai (17 million), Manila (12 million), Cairo (11 million), Bangkok (8 million) and many more have already crossed the limits of human agglomeration and management. Each year, almost 65% of the population added in the world, migrates to the cities, mostly in the less industrialized countries. These cities have become cesspools of human existence.

If the above analysis is correct, then the consequences of the increase in human population are grave: despite industrialization and the agricultural revolution, more and more people are driven to hopelessness because of the declining resources while at the same time the ecological integrity is dismembered. In such conditions there is neither justice nor are there human rights.

The conclusions are imperative: no matter what, the growth of population must be stopped at any cost and by whatever means bringing it to a sustainable level by 2010 AD. It is clear that the onus lies with the developing societies where the numbers are increasing wildly. But we would fail totally if we do not address the issue of consumerism simultaneously. After all, much of the demise of the earth has been due not only to the increasing number of humans, but also to the profuse consumption of the few.

Speaking about population control, let us recognize the work of the United Nations through its agency, The United Nations Fund for Population Activities (UNFPA). Its three major conferences — Budapest, Mexico and Cairo — have played a significant role at a global scale in bringing the problem of population to the attention of the world. The International Conference on Population and Development (ICPD) in Cairo, Egypt, in 1994 was a great event of hope despite many political and religious controversies. Many experts felt that the world was ready for taking action to stem population growth. Only recently the UNFPA organized The Hague Forum to evaluate the situation since the Cairo ICPD. Unfortunately, we are still far from reaching the replacement level. The United Nations can only do what is possible within the framework of its limited resources and the political constraints in each nation. Those of us who recognize the larger threat to humanity if we fail to stop the population growth, refuse to accept the present 1.3% annual increase in the world population. Therefore, we suggest that, at a global scale, population control should be the first priority of humanity.

Besides the global plan of action, each society should set up its own plan along with sufficient allocation of resources and specific time-bound programs. Since the governments can do only so much, we believe that population control should be part of the sustainable development programs at the grass root level. In these efforts, NGOs and social as well environmental groups must provide a vanguard.

In these efforts, every possible measure should be available either free or at the cheapest possible cost so that the poorest people can afford it. We are convinced that the one child family policy of China adopted in 1979 is the only alternative for most of the poor countries —Ethiopia, Kenya, Bangladesh, Pakistan, India and many other countries. Our proposal is that we must bring family planning education to every fertile couple in the world by 2005 A.D. We should also educate them about environmental protection and sustainable development as part of the population control programs. We emphasize here that contraceptives and all other services for family planning should be available free to people as part of their human rights. The cost of preventing a birth is much cheaper than taking care of a human being in this over-crowded world.

Every society must challenge the male domination and control of fertility. Men and women have equal right to decide and they should be treated equally. In fact, all the family planning programs in every society should be in charge of women, who have a key role to play in social development, environmental protection and population sustainability.

Speaking about social development, no religion has the business to interfere with population control programs. A woman has the right to use any method to prevent birth. We all recognize that health is a key issue in family planning, particularly the

Box 5.1. **UNFPA MOVES DAY OF SIX BILLION BASED ON NEW POPULATION ESTIMATES**

NEW YORK, 28 October 1998 — The United Nations Population Fund today announced that the Day of Six Billion, the day the world population reaches 6 billion, will be marked on 12 October 1999. The new date is based on the revised population estimate released today by the Population Division of the United Nations Department of Economic and Social Affairs. "This is very encouraging news", said Dr. Nafis Sadik, Executive Director, United Nations Population Fund. Declines in fertility levels have pushed back the date the world population will reach 6 billion people from 16 June 1999 to 12 October 1999.

"However, world population is still increasing by 78 million people a year. Ninety-seven per cent of that increase is in developing countries where access to family planning and reproductive health services is limited and where pregnancy and childbirth are still a risk to the lives and health of women", said Dr. Sadik.

The projections confirm that fertility levels in developing countries are continuing to decline. This trend is in part the result of better reproductive health and family planning services and improved education of women. There is also evidence of long-term decline to below replacement levels in most industrialized countries.

"The glass is half full", said Dr. Sadik. "We need to continue striving for women's rights to reproductive health care, including family planning, and the right of women and men to decide the size and spacing of their families. We must work to promote gender equality and equity and women's empowerment. We have come half way towards the goal of slowing overall population growth but there are no guarantees that this success will continue". Tragically, part of the slowdown in population growth, according to the new estimates, is a result of the HIV/AIDS epidemic which has a tremendous destabilizing impact on communities, families and children. In Botswana, the hardest-hit country, one adult in four is infected with HIV. According to Population Division estimates, life expectancy in Botswana is projected to fall to 41 years by 2005, 29 years less than expected in the absence of AIDS.

Nevertheless, Botswana's population is still projected to double between 1995 and 2050.

Source: 1998 Revision —World population estimates and projections

health of women and children. This implies that the investment in health contributes significantly to our efforts in family planning.

In this globalized world, in which environmental boundaries do not exist and economic boundaries are disappearing, the distribution of population is an important issue if we want to save the earth. We believe, therefore, that the movement and the settlement of people worldwide should be freely allowed. If goods and services can move unrestrained, why not people. After all, the optimum distribution of population is a necessary condition for ecological balance.

In time, if we succeed in controlling population and exaggerated consumption and we develop sustainable habitats living on minimum resources, we shall have the original balance, which has allowed evolution to continue. In such a society, there will be no burden on the ecological reserves necessary for other species to share the earth with us and for generations to come. The wilderness, where life originated and evolved, will always be there and we shall remain integrated in its fold for ever.

....

Human Domination of Earth Ecosystems

Peter M. Vitousek, Harold A Mooney, Jane Lubchenco, and Jerry M. Melillo

Man came silently into the world ... and the world ignored his coming ... in order, some million years later, to notice with all the greater amazement, the existence of a leading figure on the stage of world history, ... still unconsciously motivated by hunger, thirst and primitive instincts, armed only with teeth and a pair of strong hands, man set about changing his environment.
— Pierre Tielhard de Chardin

Human alteration of Earth is substantial and growing. Between one-third and one-half of the land surface has been transformed by human action; the carbon dioxide concentration in the atmosphere has increased by nearly 30 percent since the beginning of the Industrial Revolution; more atmospheric nitrogen is fixed by humanity than by all natural terrestrial sources combined, more than half of all accessible surface fresh water is put to use by humanity, and about one-quarter of the bird species of Earth have been driven to extinction. By these and other standards, it is clear that we live in a human-dominated planet.

All organisms modify their environment, and humans are no exception. As the human population has grown and the power of technology has expanded, the scope and nature of this modification has changed drastically. Until recently, the term "human-dominated ecosystems" would have elicited images of agricultural fields, pastures, or urban landscapes; now it applies with greater or lesser force to all of Earth. Many ecosystems are dominated directly by humanity, and no ecosystem on Earth's surface is free of pervasive human influence.

This article provides an overview of human effects on Earth's ecosystems. It is not intended as a litany of environmental disasters, though some disastrous situations are described; nor is it intended to downplay or to celebrate environmental successes, of which there have been many. Rather, we explore how large humanity looms as a presence on the globe—how, even on the grandest scale, most aspects of the structure and functioning of Earth's ecosystems cannot be understood without accounting for the strong, often dominant influence of humanity.

The growth of the human population and growth in the resource base used by humanity is maintained by a suite of human enterprises such as agriculture, industry, fishing, and international commerce. These enterprises transform the land surface (through cropping, forestry, and urbanization), alter the major bio-geochemical cycles, and add or remove species and genetically distinct populations in most of Earth's ecosystems. Many of these changes are substantial and reasonably well quantified; all are ongoing. These relatively well-documented changes in turn entrain further alterations to the functioning of the Earth system, most notably by driving global climatic change and causing irreversible losses of biological diversity.

Land Transformation

Land transformation encompasses a wide variety of activities that vary substantially in their intensity and consequences. At one extreme, 10 to 15% of Earth's land surface is occupied by row-crop agriculture or by urban-industrial areas, and another 6 to 8% has been converted to pastureland; these systems are wholly changed by human activity. At the other extreme, every terrestrial ecosystem is affected by increased atmospheric carbon dioxide (CO_2), and most ecosystems have a history of hunting and other low intensity resource extraction. Between these extremes lie grassland and semi-arid ecosystems that are grazed (and sometimes degraded) by domestic animals, and forests and woodlands from which wood products have been harvested; together, these represent the majority of Earth's vegetated surface.

The variety of human effects on land makes any attempt to summarize land transformations globally a matter of semantics as well as substantial uncertainty. Estimates of the fraction of land transformed or degraded by humanity (or its corollary, the fraction of the land's biological production that is used or dominated) fall in the range of 39 to 50%.

Overall, land transformation represents the primary driving force in the loss of biological diversity worldwide. Moreover, the effects of land transformation extend far beyond the boundaries of transformed lands. Land transformation can affect climate directly through local and even regional scales. It contributes approx. 20% to current anthropogenic CO_2 emissions, and more substantially to the increasing concentrations of the greenhouse gases methane and nitrous oxide; fires associated with it alter the reactive chemistry of the troposphere, bringing elevated carbon-monoxide concentrations and episodes of urban-like photochemical air pollution to remote tropical areas of Africa and South America; and it causes runoff of sediment and nutrients that drive substantial changes in stream, lake, estuarine, and coral reef ecosystems.

Oceans

Human alterations of marine ecosystems are more difficult to quantify than those of terrestrial ecosystems, but several kinds of information suggest that they are substantial. The human population is concentrated near coasts—about 60% within 100 km—and the oceans' productive coastal margins have been affected strongly by humanity. Coastal wetlands that mediate interactions between land and sea have been altered over large areas; for example, approximately 50% of mangrove ecosystems globally have been transformed or destroyed by human activity. Moreover, a recent analysis suggested that although humans use about 8% of the primary production of the oceans, that fraction grows to more than 25% for upwelling areas and to 35% for temperate continental shelf systems.

Many of the fisheries that capture marine productivity are focused on top predators, whose removal can alter marine ecosystems out of proportion to their abundance. Moreover, many such fisheries have proved to be unsustainable, at least at our present level of knowledge and control. As of 1995, 22% of recognized marine fisheries were overexploited or already depleted, and 44% more were at their limit of exploitation. The consequences of fisheries are not restricted to their target organisms; commercial marine fisheries around the world discard 27 million tons of non-target animals annually, a quantity nearly one-third as large as total landings. Moreover, the dredges and trawls used in some fisheries damage habitats substantially as they are dragged along the sea floor.

A recent increase in the frequency, extent, and duration of harmful algal blooms in coastal areas suggests that human activity has affected the base as well as the top of marine food chains. Harmful algal blooms are sudden increases in the abundance of marine phytoplankton that produce harmful structure of chemicals. Some but not all of these phytoplankton are strongly pigmented (red or brown tides). Algal blooms usually are correlated with changes in temperature, nutrients, or salinity; nutrients in coastal waters, in particular, are much modified by human activity. Algal blooms can cause extensive fish kills through toxins and by causing anoxia; they also lead to paralytic shellfish poisoning and amnesic shellfish poisoning in humans. Although the existence of harmful algal blooms has long been recognized, they have spread widely in the past two decades.

Alterations of the Biogeochemical Cycles

Carbon. Life on Earth is based on carbon, and the CO_2 in the atmosphere is the primary resource for photosynthesis. Humanity adds CO_2 to the atmosphere by mining and burning fossil fuels,

---

Box 6.1. **EL NINO & THE GLOBAL CLIMATE**

In the spring of 1982, a barely known volcano in Mexico called El Chichon erupted for the first time in recorded history, claimed up to 3500 lives and caused tens of thousands of people to flee their homes. Not long afterwards, scientists detected swarms of earthquakes and large submarine lava flows in the equatorial portion of the East Pacific Rise, the ridge that runs north along the Pacific floor some 1000 miles west of the Galapagos Islands. At the same time, in June, there was sudden and dramatic drop in atmospheric pressure farther south on the Rise at Easter Island, and also at Tahiti, well over 2000 miles away to the west. About a month later, weather stations on Fanning and Christmas Islands in the mid-Pacific reported an unusual rise in sea level, of 5 to 10 inches (15 to 25 cm). Simultaneously, in the western Pacific at Palau and Guadalcannal, the sea level dropped 4 to 6 inches (10 to 15 cm). Then, gradually but persistently, Pacific sea surface temperatures at the equator began to rise. Off the coast of Peru, the temperature reached over 26.5 degrees C (800 F), nearly 7 degrees C above normal. In the mid-Pacific, the temperature climbed as high as 30 degrees C (860F), a level described by one scientist as 'about as hot as the ocean can get'.

Peru's multimillion-dollar anchovy industry was devastated that year as the fish moved away; on Christmas Island, 17 million birds disappeared without a trace. During late summer, coastal areas of Ecuador and Peru began to suffer torrential rains, in some cases 300 times the normal annual rainfall. Continuing for eight months, the rains produced some of the worst floods this century. Avalanches and swollen rivers cut off scores of towns; several hundred people died. In the mid-Pacific there was an abrupt rise in typhoons: French Polynesia, which receives an average of one typhoon every 50 years, was battered by five in as many months.

Across the Pacific, in Indonesia and Australia and across the Indian

the residue of life from the distant past, and by converting forests and grasslands to agricultural and other low-biomass ecosystems. The net result of both activities is that organic carbon from rocks, organisms, and soils is released into the atmosphere as CO_2.

Ocean in southern Africa, there was unprecedented drought and famine, by contrast. In Australia, thousand of acres of farmland desiccated and turned to desert; some of the worst bush fires in the history of the world's most fire-prone country left 72 people dead, as many as 8000 people homeless, and destroyed property worth several thousand million dollars.

In due course the drought spread – to India, Sri Lanka, the Philippines, Hawaii and Mexico.

In December, it was the turn of the United States. A dozen people perished on the West Coast in storms and mudslides that smothered crops and ravaged much of California's magnificent coastal highway. In Los Angeles, a freak tornado tore through the downtown area. On the Gulf Coast, floods drove 60,000 people from their homes and killed 50. No weather like it had ever been seen before by US meteorologists.

But although they did not predict it, they were able to fit it into a certain pattern. For centuries, Peruvian fishermen have known that warm water from the Pacific periodically overlays the usual upwelling of cold plankton-rich water off Peru and deprives them of their catch, while on land, floods deprive them of their homes. Since the upset generally comes towards the end of the year, near Christmas time, the fishermen have given Nature's unwelcome gift an ironic name, El Nino ("The Child"). Looking at the records of El Nino this century, scientists can see that it has tended to follow a volcanic eruption and submarine earthquake swarms. But in their current state of knowledge of the Earth, all they can do is speculate as to whether or not major volcanic eruptions, submarine earth quakes and worldwide meteorological mayhem are connected phenomena. As Earth scientists sometimes like to remark about themselves : they are like the six blind men of Indostan who, after examining an elephant – or rather six different parts of an elephant - `disputed loud and long',/ Each in his own opinion/Exceeding stiff and strong,/ Though each was partly in the right,/ And all were in the wrong".

Source: "The Earth Shock: climate, complexity and the forces of Nature", Andrew Robinson 1993

The modern increase in CO_2 represents the clearest and best-documented signal of human alteration of the Earth system. Thanks to the foresight of Roger Revelle, Charles Keeling, and others who initiated careful, and systematic measurements of atmospheric CO_2 in 1857 and sustained them through budget crises and changes in scientific fashions, we have observed the concentration of CO_2 as it has increased steadily from 315 ppm to 362 ppm. Analysis of air bubbles extracted from the Antarctic and Greenland ice caps extends the record back much further; the CO_2 concentration was more or less stable near 280 ppm for

---

Box 6.2. **THERE GOES THE OZONE**

"What does it mean to redefine one's relationship to the sky? What will it do to our children's outlook on life if we have to teach them to be afraid to look up?"   — Vice President Al Gore

You grab sunblock number one hundred ninety-eight, three pairs of sunglasses, three umbrellas, and two hats that cover your ears.

You put on a long-sleeved shirt, pants, socks, and sandals. You get to the beach and sit there, buried under your clothing, sweating and suffocating. You feel like a caveman. You don't know why you are wearing all this stuff... a friend told you...who heard it on TV...something about skin cancer and premature wrinkling. All you know is it is no fun going to the beach anymore.

You've also heard something about the ozone. Indeed, if it weren't for what remains of the ozone layer in the sky, we'd all be fried dumplings by now. The problem is that industrial pollutants in the sky have been breaking down ozone. Since 1985, scientists have been documenting this gap in the ozone—the ozone hole—which is spreading from Antarctica to heavily populated areas. Due to this spreading hole, more of the sun's harmful ultraviolet (UV) radiation is leaking into the earth's atmosphere.

The hot news is that the ozone is about as thin as parchment paper and growing thinner with every passing year, and that this depletion is now occurring in the spring and summer, the time of the year when the sun's

thousands of years until about 1800, and has increased exponentially since then.

There is no doubt that this increase has been driven by human activity, today primarily by fossil fuel combustion. The sources of CO_2 can be traced isotopically; before the period of extensive nuclear testing in the atmosphere, carbon depleted in ^{14}C was a specific tracer of CO_2 derived from fossil fuel combustion, whereas carbon depleted in ^{13}C characterized CO_2 from both fossil fuels and land transformation. Direct measurements in the atmosphere, and analyses of carbon isotopes in tree rings, show

---

rays are the most direct and able to do the most damage. That means that we have a serious health problem—too much sun is getting through.

Did you know:

— If ozone loss reaches ten percent by the year 2000, as expected, there will be about a quarter of a million additional cases of skin cancer annually in the United States, and an estimated four thousand more deaths.

— Excess UV exposure is thought to cause cataracts. More than a million additional cases of cataracts will occur by the end of this decade because of increasing UV exposure

— There is evidence that ozone depletion is damaging people's Immune systems, harming their ability to fight infectious disease. This happens before they lose protection against sunburn. How dark the skin is doesn't seem to matter.

— One in six Americans will develop skin cancer in their lifetime. The incidence of a deadly skin cancer form of melanoma is presently rising at a faster rate than that of any other cancer. In 1935, the risk of developing melanoma in the United States during one's lifetime was one in fifteen hundred. Today it's one in one hundred and five.

— Sunbathers should not be overly confident with sunscreen. It may not protect against the growth of skin cancer that began in childhood.

Source : " Living Healthy in a Toxic World", p 118, David Steinman and R.Michael Wisner, 1996.

Box 6.3. **TRINIDAD IN A GREENHOUSE**

As permanent-looking as the surrounding blue waters, the palm-covered beaches of Trinidad are slowly shrinking. One 70-year-old man can remember playing soccer as a child where the Caribbean is now meters deep. Scientists blame sea-level-rise on changing global temperatures. The buildup of green gases (carbon dioxide, methane, CFC's) in the Earth's atmosphere may make the earth warmer, which, in turn, may cause seawater to expand and glaciers to melt. Climatologists predict that if average air temperatures rise just a few degrees, the sea level will rise from 60 to 100 centimeters (25 to 40 inches) in the near future. The impacts of sea level rise are particularly daunting for small Caribbean islands such as Trinidad and Tobago. Increasing numbers of tornadoes and sea spouts, erosion of coastlands and flooding have been documented in Trinidad and Tobago. Saltwater is introducing into coastal aquifers, threatening freshwater supplies and agricultural soils with salinization. Earthwatch teams are needed to catalog, analyze and interpret field evidence for global warming and sea level rise in the Caribbean. How are temperature and precipitation patterns changing? Are these changes affecting coastal ecosystems, such as mangrove swamps and coral reefs? How much land are the islands losing to coastal erosion?

During the past century, global mean temperature has risen by about 0.5°C and mean sea level has risen by about 10 cm. Massive increases in greenhouse gases from industrialization and forest clearing, many scientists say, have warmed the planet's atmosphere. Under this scenario, polar ice caps are melting and warmer seas are expanding, and so sea level is rising. If such global warming continues, by the middle of the next century, the Caribbean could face an additional 2°C rise in mean air temperature and 30 cm rise in mean sea level, with increased flooding, hurricanes, droughts and coral bleaching and possible salt-water contamination of aquifers. Such changes would spell disaster for the people and the agriculture and tourist-based economies of these low-lying islands.

Already, on Trinidad and Tobago, there are ominous signs that global warming may be triggering changes. Coastal erosion on the southern coast of Trinidad, for instance, eats away 2 to 4 meters of beach per year, a significant erosion rate for an island of less than 5,000 square kilometers. In the sea's wake lie abandoned buildings along the ocean, flooded coastal roadways and haphazard groins thrown up by local landowners to halt the sea's invasion. Saltwater has already contaminated some of the island's aquifers, threatening both irrigation and drinking water supplies. There seems little doubt that the sea around Trinidad and Tobago is rising, but are these changes a spin-off of global warming, or is oil or water extraction causing the islands to fall?

This past summer, for the first time on a Caribbean island, Earthwatch teams set out to objectively measure the net rate of sea-level rise and evaluate the rate and extent of coastal erosion. In addition, teams helped note, catalogue and analyze other evidence of shifts in climate, such as temperature anomalies, salinization of estuaries and aquifers, rates of siltation in mangrove swamps and possible coral bleaching.

In all, teams measured beach profiles, sampled soils and monitored salinity at 16 stations along Trinidad's coast. Travel by van and boat allowed teams to assess the amount of beach erosion around most of the island. Two of the most eroded sites were on the southwest coast. At Icacos (the southwestern tip), a long-time resident confirmed that erosion along the north and south shores had slimmed the "glossary" by 400 meters on either side while accretion on the tip had extended it by 200 meters in the past 60 years. In the process, the sea has claimed two playing fields and a cemetery. At Los Iros, the sea has eroded away a coastal road and a parking lot over the past 40 years. The shore is caving off in chunks and still-rooted, 50 year-old palm trunks lie many meters below the high-tide mark. In such places, erosion may be eating away 2-4 meters of land per year. Teams noted salinization in only one of the four aquifers tested, but pumping for water or oil extraction may be complicating the picture.

On Tobago, Earthwatch divers at Culloden Reef on the north coast recorded for the first time in preliminary dives that 80 % of elkhorn corals there were bleached at depths above 7 meters; concurrent seawater temperature reading of 27°C may be abnormally high for June. Although another diver crew at Flying Reef on the western tip of Tobago failed to note any evidence of bleaching, the consistency and extent of the bleaching at Culloden Reef indicate bleaching may be widespread and potentially a serious problem for Tobago's tourism and fishing industries.

Source : Earthwatch/UNESCO Project report 1998. Dr. Bhawan Singh, University of Montreal

that both ^{13}C and ^{14}C in CO_2 were diluted in the atmosphere relative to ^{12}C as the CO_2 concentration in the atmosphere increased. Fossil fuel combustion now adds 5.5 ± 0.5 billion metric tons of CO_2-C to the atmosphere annually, mostly in economically developed regions of the Temperate Zone. The annual accumulation of CO_2-C has averaged 3.2 ± 0.2 billion.metric tons recently.

Increased CO_2 represents the most important human enhance-ment to the greenhouse effect; the consensus of the climate research community is that it probably already affects climate detectably and will drive substantial climate change in the next century. The direct effects of increased CO_2 on plants and ecosystems may be even more important. The fact that increased CO_2 affects species differentially means that it is likely to drive substantial changes in the species composition and dynamics of all terrestrial ecosystems.

Water: Water is essential to all life. Its movement by gravity, and through evaporation and condensation, contributes to driving Earth's biogeochemical cycles and to controlling its climate. Very little of the water on Earth is directly usable by humans; most is either saline or frozen. Globally, humanity now uses more than half of the runoff water that is fresh and reasonably accessible, with about 70% of this use in agriculture. To meet increasing demands for the limited supply of fresh water, humanity has extensively altered river systems through diversions and im-poundments. In the United States, only 2% of the rivers run unimpeded, and by the end of this century, the flow of about two-thirds of all of Earth's rivers will be regulated. At present, as much as 6% of Earth's river runoff is evaporated as a consequence of human manipulations. Major rivers, including the Colorado, the Nile, and the Ganges, are used so extensively that little water reaches the sea. Massive inland water bodies, including the Aral Sea and Lake Chad, have been greatly reduced in extent by water diversions for agriculture.

Impounding and impeding the flow of rivers provides reservoirs of water that can be used for energy generation as well as for agriculture. Waterways also are managed for transport, for flood-control and for the dilution of chemical wastes. Together, these activities have altered Earth's freshwater ecosystems profoundly, to a greater extent than terrestrial ecosystems have been altered. The construction of dams affects biotic habitats indirectly as well; the damming of the Danube River, for example, has altered the silica chemistry of the entire Black Sea. The large number of operational dams (36,000) in the world, in conjunction with the many that are planned, ensure that humanity's effects on aquatic biological systems will continue. Where surface water is sparse or over-exploited, humans use groundwater—and in many areas the groundwater that is drawn upon is nonrenewable, or fossil water. For example, three-quarters of the water supply of Saudi Arabia currently comes from fossil water.

Nitrogen: Nitrogen (N) is unique among the major elements required for life, in that its cycle includes a vast atmospheric reservoir (N_2) that must be fixed (combined with carbon, hydrogen, or oxygen) before it can be used by most organisms. The supply of this fixed N controls (at least in part) the productivity, carbon storage, and species composition of many ecosystems. Before the extensive human alteration of the N cycle, 90 to 130 million metric tons of N (Tg N) were fixed biologically on land each year; rates of biological fixation in marine systems are less certain, but perhaps as much was fixed there.

Human activity has altered the global cycle of N substantially by fixing N_2—deliberately for fertilizer and inadvertently during fossil fuel combustion. Industrial fixation of N fertilizer increased from <1050Tg/year (Tg=Teragrams=10^{12}gms) in 1950 to 80 Tg/

year in 1990; after a brief dip caused by economic dislocations in the former Soviet Union, it is expected to increase to >135 Tg/year by 2030. Cultivation of soybeans, alfalfa and other legume crops that fix N symbiotically enhances fixation by another ~40 Tg/year, and fossil fuel combustion puts>20 Tg/year of reactive N into the atmosphere globally—some by fixing N_2, more from the mobilization of N in the fuel. Overall, human activity adds at least as much fixed N to terrestrial ecosystems as do all natural sources combined, and it mobilizes >50 Tg/ year more during land transformation.

Alteration of the N cycle has multiple consequences. In the atmosphere, these include (i) an increasing concentration of the greenhouse gas nitrous oxide globally; (ii) substantial increases in fluxes of reactive N gases (two-thirds or more of both nitric oxide and ammonia emissions globally are human-caused); and (iii) a substantial contribution to Acid rain and to the photochemical smog, that afflicts urban and agricultural areas throughout the world.

Synthetic organic chemicals: Synthetic organic chemicals have brought humanity many beneficial services. However, many are toxic to humans and other species, and some are hazardous in concentrations as low as 1 part per billion. Many chemicals persist in the environment for decades; some are both toxic and persistent. Long-lived organochlorine compounds provide the clearest examples of environmental consequences of persistent compounds. Insecticides such as DDT and its relative, and industrial compounds like polychlorinated biphenyls (PCBs), were used widely in North America in the 1950s and 1960s. They were transported globally, accumulated in organisms, and magnified in concentration through food chains; they devastated populations of some predators (notably falcons and eagles) and entered parts of the human food supply in concentrations higher than was prudent. Domestic use of these compounds was phased out in the 1970s in the United States and Canada and their concentrations declined thereafter. However, PCBs in particular remain readily detectable in many organisms, sometimes approaching thresholds of public health concern. They will continue to circulate through organisms for many decades.

Biotic Changes

Human modification of Earth's biological resources—its species and genetically distinct populations—is substantial and growing. Extinction is a natural process, but the current rate of loss of genetic variability, of populations, and of species is far above background rates; it is ongoing; and it represents a wholly irreversible global change. At the same time, human transport of species around the Earth is homogenizing Earth's biota, introducing many species into new areas where they can disrupt both natural and human systems.

Losses: Rates of extinction are difficult to determine globally, in part because the majority of species on Earth have not yet been identified. Nevertheless, recent calculations suggest that rates of species extinction are now to the order of 100 to 1000 times those before humanity's dominance of the Earth. At present, 11% of the remaining birds, 18% of mammals, 5% of fish, and 8% of plant species on Earth are threatened with extinction. There has been a disproportionate loss of large mammal species because of hunting; these species played a dominant role in many ecosystems, and their loss has resulted in a fundamental change in the dynamics of those systems, one that could lead to further extinction. The largest organisms in marine systems have been affected similarly, by fishing and whaling.

Invasions: In addition to extinction, humanity has caused a rearrangement of Earth's biotic systems, through the mixing of floras and faunas that had long been isolated geographically. The magnitude of the transport of species, termed "biological invasion", is enormous; invading species are present almost everywhere. On many islands, more than half of the plant species are non–indigenous, and in many continental areas the figure is 20% or more.

As with extinction, biological invasion occurs naturally—and as with extinction, human activity has accelerated its rate by orders of magnitude. Many biological invasions are effectively irreversible; once replicating biological material is released into the environment

---

Box 6.4. I HAVE ONE WORD FOR YOU - PLASTIC

It's hard being a disco girl in the 90s. Sally's one consolation for working at Jimmy's Second Hand Music Store is getting all her Donna Summer disco CDs at half price. It's tough working the shrink-wrap machine, standing all day in white, patent leather disco boots, trying to make scuzzy, used CDs look like they're worth Jimmy's outrageous prices. At least, she doesn't have to worry about sitting down in her vinyl miniskirt while Joe the Lech drools across the floor. Sally's three-inch acrylic nails snag in the machine all day.

At lunchtime she grabs her pink plastic Barbie lunchbox and makes a beeline to her car—a pink '69 Corvette. It is a really nice car. Sally protects the leather with see-through seat covers. They're a little hot as she plops down. Ouch! But she jams in her Donna Summer CD and it wails on her eight-speaker stereo. Life is good. Its down to the "drive-thru" for her coffee and then to the park where she can eat in peace and dream of line-dancing with the Bee Gees. She hates these coffee cups, though. The stuff just sweats through the sides and drips all over the place. She hates the sandwich bags more—they're bitch to open with three-inch nails. She squirts down a soft drink from her 7-11 souvenir sports bottle, and checks her watch. It's almost time for her doctor's appointment. You have to stay in shape if you want to be a disco girl!

When she arrives, her doctor looks concerned. "Sally, your cholesterol's perfect, but your blood is half plastic!"

"Oh," she says, unbothered. She's got something more important on her mind, rubbing her arm, then her leg. "Doctor, is this really my skin?" Styrene is a plastic chemical found in literally every American. Styrene is

and becomes successful there, calling it back is difficult and expensive at best. Moreover, some species introductions have consequences. Some degrade human health and that of other species. Finally, some invasions drive losses in the biological diversity of native species and populations; after land transformation, they are the next most important cause of extinction.

Conclusions

The global consequences of human activity are not something to face in the future—they are with us now. All of these changes

associated with a range of disorders including cancer, nerve damage, fatigue, and loss of memory How'd it get there? How about those fast-food cups and containers?

Plastic provides enormous benefits and makes life easier. Ask an athlete wearing protective headgear, a heart valve patient, or anybody leaving Blockbuster on a Friday night, arms filled with videos and CDs. But we don't need plastic everything.

Do you know:

— NASA banned the use of polyvinyl chloride in space capsules because of toxic fumes

— Recycle plastics, sure! But that's not the health problem. Manufacturing plastics is one of the largest sources of toxic wastes. They pollute our air, water, land—and us!

— Other plastics used in food packaging leach cancer-causing chemicals into food and beverages.

Simple things to do

— Don't eat or drink out of polystyrene ("Styrofoam") containers.

— Buy fresh foods. Avoid plastic food packaging when you can.

— Tell store clerks you don't need a bag when you don't.

— Tell the dry cleaner to "hold" on the plastic wrap. It traps the dry-cleaning chemicals on your clothes, and those chemicals then concentrate in your closet. Or use the protective wrap until you get home and remove it and let your clothes air out on the porch, balcony, or in the garage before putting them away.

Source: "Living Healthy in a toxic World", p110 David Steinman and R. Michael Wisner, 1996.

are ongoing, and in many cases accelerating; many of them were entrained long before their importance was recognized. Moreover, all of these seemingly disparate phenomena trace to a single cause—the growing scale of the human enterprise. The rates, scales, kinds and combinations of changes occurring now are fundamentally different from those at any other time in history; we are changing Earth more rapidly than we are understanding it. We live on a human-dominated planet—and the momentum of human population growth, together with the imperative for further economic development in most of the world, ensures that our dominance will increase. We cannot escape responsibility for managing the planet. Our activities are causing rapid, novel and substantial changes to earth's ecosystems. Maintaining populations, species and ecosystems in the face of those changes and maintaining the flow of goods and services they provide humanity will require active management for the foreseeable future.

....

Of Pipedreams, Science and Wilderness

R. F. Muller

*No one is going to repeal the second law of
thermodynamics. Not even the democrats.*
—Kenneth Boulding

They have done it again! The technocrats have a new plan to
reprogram our world. Consider the age-old dream of our species,
the dream of control over nature without any drawbacks. Well,
they think they finally have it and it's called "nanotechnology".

This was revealed in an interview of MIT zealots on National
Public Radio on June 24 of this year(1987). The prefix 'nano'
means "very small" and in this case refers to ordering
manipulations on an atomic scale. They are not just talking about
the natural and spontaneous ordering or disordering of atoms in
crystals as a response to temperature changes (a field in which
I once did research), which has numerous scientific and
technological applications in its own right. What they mean is
the deliberate multiscale ordering of the world from atoms on up!

But there is a catch—the same catch that has plagued all
technological megaprojects, yet is almost never mentioned. The
catch is that to achieve some megatechnological result, certain
scientific principles must be ignored as assiduously as others are
applied. It will come as no surprise that one body of these ignored
principles is the science of ecology, but curiously, another is that
brainchild of the industrial revolution itself, classical thermodynamics. Of course, thermodynamics is not ignored entirely,
because no significant technological device or process can be
achieved without taking it into account. The rub is that our
technologically optimistic friends always stop with the technology

as such and do not include the "externals", with which the technology necessarily interacts—environmental thermodynamics if you will.

Environmentalists are deeply suspicious of science. But whether science is ultimately good or disastrous for the planet (and I am strongly tempted to believe the latter) isn't a useful question here because science appears to be an inevitable product of a species that the planet is stuck with temporarily. So we might as well make the best of a bad situation by at least ensuring that critical rules of the game like those of ecology and thermodynamics are not disregarded.

Thermodynamics as represented by its first and second "laws"

Box 7.1. RADIOACTIVE WASTES: AN ASPIRIN TABLET PER PERSON?

It is not uncommon to hear from the public relation arm of the Nuclear Industry that the radioactive wastes from nuclear power are equivalent in size to only an aspirin tablet per year for every person whose electricity is provided by nuclear plants. Probably, the most misleading analogy is that toxicity, not volume, is the important characteristics of those wastes. If a tablet were to be an apt comparison, it would have to be a cyanide tablet - & even that would not do justice to the actual toxicity of the fission products.

It turns out, moreover that 1 tablet per person is far from a correct figure, even in respect to volume. If the high level radioactive wastes to be solidified in their most concentrated form (the form to which the aspirin tablet view presumably refers), the resulting volume per 1000 MWe LWR per year would be 2.5 to 3.0 cubic meters. Since such a plant running at a generous average of 75% of full capacity could meet the full electricity demand (home, commerce & industry) of 750,000 Americans in 1975, the volume of high level of solid waste per person served would be 3.3 to 4.0 cubic centimeters. The volume of an aspirin tablet is 0.4 cu.cm., so the solidified high-level wastes would be about the size of 10 aspirin tablets per person.

That, however, is only the tip of the iceberg. Most high level

is the science of the possible and the impossible, a discipline that sets severe limits as well as serving indispensably in the development of technology. It is also well grounded in experience so that we know that no proposed industrial chemical reaction or physical process for which unfavorable thermodynamic numbers are obtained is possible unless it is driven by some external process; and these external processes are usually prohibitively costly in monetary and environmental terms. To illustrate, the frequently proposed use of water as a source of hydrogen chemical fuel would require a fearsome input of energy from another source, such as nuclear fission, to separate the hydrogen from oxygen—much more energy would be required

wastes have not been solidified yet & federal law requires only that such solidification take place within 10 years of the creation of the wastes. The volume of the liquid form before solidification is 10 times greater than that of solid (therefore we would have 100 aspirin tablets per person). Additionally there are the highly radioactive remains of the fuel cladding (2.0 cu.cm. per reactor or 5 more aspirin tablets per persons)

There is still more. The reprocessing plants also produces annually for every 1000 MWe reactor about 25 cu.cm. of intermediate level liquid wastes (contaminated to between 10,000 & 1 million times the maximum permissible concentration.) & 1200 cu.cm. of low level. These wastes would amount to 60 & 3000 additional aspirin tablets per person respectively. Low level solid wastes from the reprocessing plant and from the reactor itself amount to between 80 & 160 cu.cm. per year (200-400 more aspirin tablet per person). And those wastes contain alpha emitting radioisotopes of very long half-life. All this adds up to a volume equal to that of between 3300 & 3600 aspirin tablets per year per person served.

It is disquieting, in any case, to find persons in the nuclear industry – so quick to complain about what its representatives consider to be irresponsible statements from environmentalists – glibly dispensing information that is both qualitatively misleading and quantitatively by a factor of thousands.

(MWe: Mega watts of electricity ; LWR : Light water reactors).

Source : ERDA, Alternatives for managing wastes from reactors & post fission operation in the LWR fuel cycle.

than the hydrogen could ever yield.

Some will recall the first law as the rather prosaic statement that energy can't be created or destroyed as long as its equivalence to mass is recognized. The second law, which is more mysterious and pertinent to our problem states that the disorder or "entropy" of any isolated system always spontaneously increases. In practical terms this means that although we can create technological order in local parts of the environment (e.g., an industrial site), a concomitant greater quantity of disorder will be created, inevitably not only at that site, but in external regions from which ordering elements such as energy and materials are drawn. This is a game that can't be won (as I have argued in past articles: Thermodynamics of Environmental Degradation, NASA document X-644-71-121, 1971; Science 196,261,1977,etc).

Similar conclusions were reached by Nicholas Georgescu-Roegen with respect to economics (The Entropy Law and the Economic Process, Cambridge, MA. 1971, and other publications). However, the whole topic of environmental thermodynamics has been shunned by the technocrats because they consider it a "Bad News Science". From this we can infer that thermodynamics can be as powerful an ally for us as is ecology. It is, in fact, the purely physical basis for the so-called "laws of ecology" and is equally applicable to every aspect of society in which energy is involved.

In a not too remote tomorrow the dreamers of nanotechnology would attempt to order large segments of our world from the atomic level on up, to create unprecedented control of chemical, mechanical and biologic systems by fitting every individual atom into a predesignated framework to achieve a technological paradise. To get a feel for the magnitude of such a program, consider our everyday experiences in which the same thermodynamic forces are at work. We all know how difficult it is to order our lives, simply to keep our dwellings neat and our personal effects in place. Note that we are talking here of our familiar macroscopic world. Imagine then trying to reduce the underlying microscopic world, vibrant and nascent, to this same brand of preconceived anthropocentric order!

We have seen that by the second law, every ordered region we create calls into being an even greater region of disorder as a result of the increased energy flux. In environmental terms this technological energy, no matter how benign its origin, is synonymous with pollution. Even the most advanced microelectronic and solar energy systems, which were once regarded as "pollution free", are subject to the same energy degradation as are the crudest factories and mines, except the degradation may take different forms (Muller, Environmental Action 10, 15, 1978). If then by any chance—and this chance is small—the technocrats were able to order our entire planetary surface to create the wonder world of their dreams, the energy required and the resulting pollution might well be enough to disorder much of the solar system!

I won't tire you with the familiar and dreary litany of technological failures—all of them routed as examples of our "control" over nature—that are devastating this beautiful planet. However, it's useful to note in passing a few familiar cases that may not strike everyone as offensive.

Consider current attempts at super-control in the medical profession in which ever more "sophisticated technologies", such as organ transplants and complex life support systems, are being developed. Then be aware that burgeoning material requirements and costs of these technologies are driving the costs of ordinary health care beyond the range of those people (externals!) who will never need the new technology. Or consider the practice of "advanced societies" and particularly the US, of keeping thousands of square miles of terrain in a technological straight jacket at enormous cost in labor, energy and materials. This applies

Box 7.2. THE ENVIRONMENT, THE MILITARY AND WOMEN'S HEALTH

As human beings, our health and well-being depends upon a number of factors, not least of which is a healthy environment. When the environment becomes contaminated with toxic substances, it can have a serious impact on the health of nearby populations. This has been the case in French Polynesia where, since 1963, not less than 167 nuclear weapons tests have been conducted on the atolls of Moruroa and Fangataufa. Of these tests, forty-four were conducted in the atmosphere, subjecting the region to significant quantities of nuclear fall-out.

Although testing has been conducted underground since 1974, dangers to health, to the environment, and to the socio-economic well–being of the Polynesians persists. As with other areas of the world where nuclear tests have been conducted, few reliable statistics are available as evidence of the grave impact that nuclear activities have had on the environment and, through extension, on human health. Publication of public health records was suspended soon after testing began. Although there is no statistical proof, the people of Moruroa know that there are too many miscarriages, too many stillbirths and 'jellyfish' babies, too many birth defects, too many cancers and illness...

Military activity is often overlooked as a source of environmental degradation and, by extension, the deterioration of human health. The following story illustrates the impact that one form of military activity, nuclear testing, has had upon the people of French Polynesia. This is one woman's story - this is Tiare's story:

In 1974, Tiare, a Tahitian woman now in her early 30's fell in love with a young man, Peni, of the same age. In the Polynesian way she went to live with Peni in his parent's home and soon become pregnant, eventually giving birth to a well-shaped and healthy daughter named Tina. But life was already becoming difficult for all Tahitians due to the arrival of more than 15,000 French troops and settelers. Peni began looking for a job to pay a share of the rapidly increasing living costs of the family.

The only well paid job he could find was as an unskilled civilian worker on the nuclear test site at Moruroa atoll, 1,200 km from Tahiti. The only opportunities he had to see his family from then on was during the two to three days leave that all the Polynesian workers at the Moruroa were entitled to each month.

Peni's work consisted of collecting garbage of all kinds, including contaminated clothing shed by the technicians at the test site and the dead fish that would float in the lagoon after each nuclear test. Often, after having burnt the garbage in a pit, he had to climb down into the pit to clear it, barefoot, with no gloves or protective clothing.

During the following ten years, Tiare gave birth to four more children. Her second daughter Moana, born in 1977, was in poor health from birth but it was not until she was four months old that the doctor discovered that she had an enlarged liver. In 1979, she had her first boy, Nui. He suffered from meningitis and despite medical treatment he suffered mental instability.

A year later, Tiare was pregnant again. Prenatal problems lasted for five months, until a premature baby was born. The hospital nurse told her that the child was alive, but when Tiare and Peni, very naturally wanted to see their child , they were told by the French doctors that it had died and were only shown a photograph of a foetus. In January 1986, Tiare gave birth to another boy, Manu, who seemed to be in good health but was born without an anus. Tiare has been sent with Manu to France for surgery. She had her last child, a daughter, in 1987.

It was a terrible period of problems, worries and suffering for Tiare and Peni. By 1987, Peni, who had worked for eleven years at the Moruroa nuclear test site, asked to be transferred to the army camp in Tahiti, so he could look after his family better, especially when his wife was absent with Manu in France. Manu is now four and a half years old and is once again in France for extended medical treatment. He hopes that he will soon be able to return to Tahiti and begin schooling, as he is no longer urinating all the time which, up to now, has made it necessary for him to wear diapers.

This is a true account of one family's tragic experience with the effects of nuclear radiation on human health. They do not represent a 'statistical glitch.' Their story is not unique, it is replicated to a lesser or greater extent in many families in French Polynesia.

Note: the names of the family members have been changed to protect them from reprisals.

Source : Women's International league for Peace and Freedom "Women and the environment", edited by Annabel Rodda.

not only to the monotonous monocultures of agri business, but particularly to the trimmed, herbicide and pesticide-saturated yards, roadsides and other artificially vegetated areas that are dedicated to nothing more than a perverted aesthetic ideal willed to us by English lords. Add to these the inefficient estates of hobby agriculture that enslave more thousands of square miles as well as the large expanses of public land devoted to deficit timber, grazing and mining operations by the federal government. Finally, wonder, that even the most nature-alienated MIT technocrat, confronted seasonally by his own crabgrass, could consider nanotechnology seriously.

What we have here is luxury feeding on necessity, the long-term consequences of which may be illustrated, according to Georgescu-Roegen, by the production of Cadillacs which will inevitably preclude the availability of plowshares to future generations (Southern Economic Journal 41, 347, 1975).

All this allows us to see wilderness in a new light. Wilderness, it appears, is the manifestation of harmony between order and disorder, both of which are necessary to maintain it. (Perhaps it is also nature's paradigm for the resolution of the contradiction between order and anarchy). The natural dispersal of seeds, for example, is a disordering process, as is the chemical diffusion of nutrients (positive change in entropy on mixing), but there is no better example of order than the adaptive survival of seedlings in specific sites.

In this scheme without a schemer, the life order created spontaneously through evolution as a response to geologic conditions and the solar flux is always exceeded by the sum of the disordering effects of decay, heat dissipation etc.; and it is this surplus disorder that drives the entire process. Part of this spontaneously expressed scheme, which is inherent in the chemistry of the system, is the enormous biologic diversity, the place-identity mosaic, which confers stability to the biosphere.

However, this stability is threatened when any species becomes dominant and attempts to exert its own form of order, usurping the environmental mosaic and decreasing diversity. In the case of our species, this usurpation, acting through both excessive numbers and high energy technology, creates disorder of the type that clashes with natural order. Consequently, the interaction of technology and nature is only a vulgar parody of the pre-existing harmony.

It is obvious that pure wilderness terrain requires no inputs of technological energy or materials to maintain it. Using an analogy from physics, wilderness may be regarded as an energy "ground state". The technological energy required to deviate greatly from this state, even to accommodate existing human numbers under minimal living standards, let alone the flaunting of luxury, places in peril our long-term survival and that of all other species.

Modern cities and agriculture necessarily displaced wilderness to accommodate the needs of excess population. However, it is becoming increasingly apparent that large tracts of wilderness—larger than those presently existing–are themselves more necessary than ever, as reservoirs of environmental amenities needed to support civilization's artifacts.

The foregoing is one of a number of possible "scientific" interpretations of the planetary dilemma, although one that is unlikely to be embraced by the scientific establishment with its demands for upbeat predictions of the conquest of nature. But at best science is only one facet of the real world—which is certainly mystical and poetic at its core. Yet, given the inevitability of its presence in our lives, our efforts must be directed toward elevating science to a new analytical level, to a system approach that recognizes the great panorama of biology, the limits set by thermodynamics and above all the unity and parity of all life forms.

At present wilderness is still regarded as basically inhospitable to the human intellect, the great chaos out of which we are elevating ourselves to unlimited heights of technological grandeur. Contrarily, central to the new level of scientific consciousness is the recognition of the wilderness source of our intellect and the continuing dependency of our intellect on wilderness, a dependency that all our high energy ordering schemes, our gleaming spaceships, cannot supplant. Finally, the new scientific consciousness also recognizes that wilderness is the life sustaining environment.

At this new level we give up the old pipedream of technological control over nature and see that what we now think of as control is only interaction and impact and that for each impact we direct at nature we are impacted in return. Only by accepting as our standard of reference the natural regimen of harmony between order and disorder – as best represented by the wilderness– can catastrophe be avoided.

....

"It would be a tragedy if
the sunrise of technology were to
be the sunset of Mankind."

— *Winston Churchill*
"Throwaway" Society.

The Age of Democratic Luxury

Theodore Roszak

*My riches consist not in the extent of my possessions
but in the fewness of my wants.*

— *J. Brotherton*

Standard economics is right, however, when it reminds us that
a flourishing supply implies an expanding demand. The Third
World would not be producing frivolous junk if the First World
did not provide so gleeful a market for it. That fact raises another,
deeper issue. Ask anybody on the street if they really need a neon
telephone; what answer would you expect to receive? Most likely
a unanimous "not at all." But ask again after they have seen a
neon telephone or two, and they might—some of them—
sheepishly confess that, while they don't actually need such an
item, it just might be "fun" to own one. "Fun" covers a great deal
of economic territory in affluent societies. It sells a lot of
merchandise. Fun movies, fun clothes, fun cosmetics, fun food
... why not fun telephones? Fun—meaning impulse buying
relished as much for the impulse as for the buying—delivers a
sense of well-being, a small touch of luxury. It makes shopping
one of the staple entertainments of our time. Always another cute
little novelty, another quirky gizmo, another fad or fashion to
bring home and talk about.

In times past, only the elite could afford to squander the
wealth of the nation. It was done as a spectator sport for the
toiling masses to see and perhaps vicariously enjoy. From a
strictly environmental viewpoint, one might almost say that an
aristocratic social order makes ecological sense. It limits
prodigality to an affordable few. The penurious majority dare not
waste, lest it go to bed each night wanting. If the neon telephone
were marketed only to a narrow elite, the biosphere could easily

budget the excess. But what if neon telephones are to be produced and consumed by the millions? Even cut-rate luxuries may be more than the earth can provide, if they must be provided on a democratic basis.

Lester Brown of the Worldwatch Institute has defined the goal of the environmental movement as sustainability, by which he means "the capacity to satisfy current needs without jeopardizing the prospects of future generations". But who is to define "current needs"? At the level of physical needs, nutritionists and medical doctors can specify the criteria of health with some assurance. But at a certain point, economics borders on psychology, and there the objective criteria are much less clear. We cross that line when we probe any consumer demand that goes beyond physical necessity. How do wants at that level become needs? The question transcends industrial societies. Among tribal groups living in far more reduced material circumstances, the potlatch provides a ceremonial opportunity to squander, even destroy wealth. The wealth has been saved up for that very reason; the act of wasting it confers social status. The occasion, a ritualized blowout, is enjoyed by all as an experience of uproarious extravagance.

With the advent of industrialism, at least through the period of primitive accumulation, the chance to experience such extravagance was significantly diminished for working millions––but only for a few generations. Eventually, the privation became both intolerable and unnecessary. Phase two of every industrial economy is the pay-off when consumption becomes not simply a pleasure but a duty. The need to move the goods becomes so pressing that ingenious method must be invented to enhance the hunger for more. An advertising industry is created to stimulate consumption, lest the system grind to a halt. But once our human weakness of frivolous, high-spirited expenditure comes to be joined to the massive productive power of an industrial system, we are clearly in for trouble sooner or later.

The classic imagery of early industrialism was that of sweated labor and grinding exploitation. There is no question but that the infrastructure of the capitalist economies was wrung from a powerless proletariat that was expected to function as nothing more than the "hands" of the system. But one generation after Marx died, something very different was being required of the workforce: the duty of compulsive consumption. Entrepreneurs like Henry Ford readily acknowledged that they had become dependent on the capacity of their workers to afford the tin lizzies they were producing. Today in societies where many still lack for the necessities, there is an appetite for "fun" merchandise that can make the demand for neon telephones as fierce as the demand for bare subsistence ever was. There are no wretched of the Earth any longer who live so remote from a movie theater, a television set, a VCR that they have not been treated to scenes of people like themselves in the developed societies wallowing in abundance. They see it, they want it, they need it. Amenities that were unimaginable for the workhouse rabble of Marx's day have become commonplace priorities around the world.

The passion to have, to own, indeed to waste, is more than mindless extravagance. Consumer egalitarianism is clearly the inevitable adjunct of political equality. In the modern world, an inalienable right to the pursuit of happiness has come to include a universal claim upon discretionary income. Emphasize the "discretionary." That has become the crucial distinction between equality as an individual political right and uniformity as a collective economic condition. Even in prosperous societies like Britain and the Scandinavian countries, taxation at a level that eliminates a certain margin of discretionary spending, no matter how capricious, has led to middle-class taxpayer revolts against the welfare establishment. Not, in all cases, because of simple greed, but because the ability to pick and choose in an open market, to buy

Box 8.1. REDUCING CONSUMPTION

Purchase less

Ask yourself whether you really need more stuff.

Avoid buying things you don't need or won't use.

Use items as long as possible (and don't replace them just because some new gizmo becomes available).

Use the library instead of purchasing every book you read.

Make gifts from materials already on hand, or give nonmaterial gifts.

Avoid excess packaging

Carry reusable bags when shopping and refuse bags for small purchases.

Buy items in bulk or with minimal packaging; avoid single-serving foods.

Choose packaging that can be recycled or reused.

Don't use disposable items

Use cloth diapers, napkins, handkerchieves and towels

Bring a washable cup to meetings; use washable plates and utensils rather than single-use items.

Buy pens, razors, flashlights and cameras with replaceable parts.

Choose items built to last and have them repaired; you will save materials and energy while providing jobs in your community.

Conserve energy

Walk, bicycle or use public transportation

Turn off (or avoid turning on) lights, water, heat and air conditioning when possible.

Put up clotheslines or racks in the backyard or basement to avoid using a clothes dryer.

Carpool and combine trips to reduce car mileage.

Save water

Water lawns and gardens only when necessary.

Use water-saving devices and fewer flushes with toilets.

Don't leave water running when washing hands, food, dishes and teeth.

Source : Environment, 1995 version, Peter Raven, Linda Berg and George Johnson.

a luxury or two brings with it a sense of freedom and dignity.

Of necessity, a democratic social order must be an ecological order; and the truer the democracy (meaning the more authentically accessible the power and the goods) the more real must the collective ecological intelligence of the society be. The standards of consumption set by aristocrats and the early industrial bourgeoisie simply cannot be extended to societies *en masse*. Rather, the desires that undergird those standards—the craving for specialness, distinction, personal worth—must be uncovered, examined, reshaped. The aspiration must be peeled down to its essence. In practical environmental terms, what does it mean (in the words of the old populist slogan) to proclaim "every man a king?"

....

The King in a carriage may ride,
And the beggar may travel at the side;
But in the general race'
They are travelling all the same pace.

— *Chronomors*

Chemical Reaction

Ann Misch

As crude as the cave man's club, the chemical
barrage has been hurled against the fabric of life.
— Rachel Carson, Silent Spring

In the giddy, early days of this century's Chemical Age, companies such as Union Carbide and Dow trumpeted the miraculous powers of chemicals ("Better Living Through Chemicals") on billboards and in ad campaigns. And chemicals did bring miracles, from antibiotics, penicillin, and other medical advances to a range of creature comforts our ancestors could never have imagined: synthetic fibers, dry cleaning, spoil-proof food, crop-saving pesticides, contraceptives, contact lenses...the list is endless. All in all, scientists have heaped more than 70,000 new chemical compounds on the bandwagon of progress, creating every imaginable convenience—and chasing every imagined ache or emptiness from our lives.

But these new creations have generated, along with all their benefits, a long list of problems, including serious health consequences. Our enthusiasm for new chemicals and the products and services they make possible has outstripped our attention to their long-term effects. While billions of dollars have been lavished on product development, marketing, promotion, and advertising, very little has been devoted to observing chemicals' interactions with living things and the environment. And these effects can never be thoroughly tested; the sheer number of combinations these chemicals now represent—in our food, water, clothing, and homes—are astronomical.

The research that has been done on chemicals' health effects has led environmental health experts to one fairly solid conclusion: there is an indisputable link between exposure to some industrial substances and certain serious diseases, particularly cancer. But some scientists are now beginning to look beyond the obvious—cancer and other easily diagnosable problems—to other health consequences of the Chemical Age. What they are finding puts a different face on the miraculous claims that we accepted without question in a more innocent era.

In the summer of 1991, a group of American scientists and other experts met at the Wingspread conference center in Racine, Wisconsin, to talk about what was still just a hunch to each of them: was it possible that the chemicals encountered in people's everyday routines—from weed killer and bug spray to chemical-laced meat and dairy products—could be causing subtle but potent health problems other than cancer?

While it is now widely accepted that certain diseases may result from exposure to hazardous substances—leukemia has been linked to benzene, an ingredient in gasoline, for example, and mesothelioma, a form of cancer, is considered a signature of asbestos exposure—the Wingspread scientists have continued to collect evidence that chemicals cause systemic damage by disrupting the functions of the endocrine system, which defends the body against infectious disease and cancer and the nervous system. Lowered fertility, abnormal sexual development, eccentric behavior, and lowered resistance to disease were among the health effects the scientists at Wingspread observed in wildlife and laboratory animals. Because most of the damage was so insidious, the scientists determined that similar effects in people might go unnoticed unless researchers specifically hunted for them. At the end of its meeting, the group called for a major epidemiological study to better assess the extent of subtle chemical damage to human health.

Some new advances in toxicology suggest that chemicals need not cause outright disease in order to have dramatic consequences. Other findings shed light on the potency of tiny exposures, and the extreme sensitivity of the developing foetus to chemicals. Since regulation of toxic chemicals has often been aimed strictly at preventing cancer and overt poisoning in adults, many subtle chemical effects on development, hormone regulation, the immune system, the nervous system, and reproduction have never been studied. "Our fascination with cancers had led us to underestimate (chemical's) other health effects," says Theo Colborn, a World Wildlife Fund zoologist who helped organize the Wingspread conference.

The Chemical Load

Society has understood for centuries the dangers posed by many natural and synthetic substances, often through casual observation of diseases that have beset workers in various "dirty" industries. Lead's dangers, for example, were recognized by the Greeks and Romans. Hippocrates noted cases of lead poisoning among miners in the fourth century B. C. Dioscerides, a Greek physician, reported in the second century, B. C., that "lead makes the mind give way." In the late 18th century, Sir Percival Pott, an Englishman, traced a connection between cancer of the scrotum, a hallmark of the profession of chimney sweeping, and the soot in the chimneys the sweeps scrubbed clean. Before their profession was outlawed for humanitarian reasons late in the 19th century, sweeps wedged themselves down soot-lined chimneys and in the process collected particles of cancer-causing coal tar in the creases and crevices of their bodies.

But by the early 1900s, modern industry was well on its way to surpassing the 19th-century industrialists' wildest dreams of progress, and in turn, chemical threats were crossing the boundaries of factories into everyday life. Industry had begun to produce synthetic chemicals by the 1920s, and some of these new chemical products, such as the notorious polychlorinated biphenyls—now commonly known as PCBs—eventually began to leach into the environment.

PCBs, first introduced in the United States in 1930 and then banned in the United States, Canada and other industrialized countries beginning in the mid-1970s, were used for decades in electrical transformers, plastics, paints, varnishes, and waxes. By the 1950s, industry had invented formulas for thousands of important industrial compounds, some of which were as-yet-unrecognized toxins.

Among the toxic compounds were a number that contained chlorine, a building block in the production of many synthetic chemicals. In its gaseous form, chlorine proved useful to the chemical industry since it bonds readily with carbon. Between 1920 and 1990, U.S. production of chlorine rose tenfold, and it now figures at roughly 11 million metric tons a year—a little less than one-third of world production.

Unfortunately, thanks to their chlorinecarbon bonds, many industrial compounds are quite stable and only break down slowly. These "organochlorine" substances are not water-soluble but do dissolve in fat. Like iron filings drawn to a magnet, these substances migrate to the reserves of fat stored in the tissues of fish, birds, mammals, and people.

In addition to creating brand-new-hazards, 20th-century industry has coaxed many naturally toxic substances from rock and soil for use in manufacturing, and in the process released them into the environment. Industry's reliance on these metals has pushed more than 300 times as much lead, 20 times as much cadmium, and four times as much arsenic into the atmosphere than is naturally present. Roughly 13 million pounds of mercury drop from the atmosphere to the earth annually in rainfall, mostly as a result of industrial activity. Mercury readily evaporates, escaping into the atmosphere. Since minute quantities of cadmium, lead, and mercury have proved poisonous to the central nervous system, their potential impact is great.

No matter how far removed from the centers of industrial activity, people have been unable to escape exposure to this chemical brew. PCBs and DDT, for example, can be detected in the soil and in the bodies of wild animals almost anywhere in the world, as well as in people living in regions of the world still untouched by industry.   Native American women living in Canada's Hudson Bay area carry roughly 3.6 parts per million of PCBs in their breast milk, compared to the one part-per-million average in industrialized countries. These women have such high PCB levels because they have diets heavy in marine mammals and

---

Box 9.1. SAFE? WHO'S KIDDING WHO?

— DDT, PCBs, chlordane, kepone, asbestos, silicone breast Implants, and leaded gasoline were all once proclaimed safe by government and industry, but later banned due to adverse health effects including cancer, nerve damage, and birth defects.

— Eighty percent of the industrial chemicals used today have had no toxicity testing.

— While meat is one of the greatest sources of pesticide exposure in your diet, the United States Department of Agriculture, responsible for food safety, tests only one out of every two hundred and fifty thousand slaughtered animals for toxic residues.

— Even after being shown to cause cancer, diethylstilbestrol (DES), which causes rare vaginal cancers in women, was used for some forty years to hasten the weight gain of cattle. It was found at levels in the food supply known to cause cancer in rodents. Today, DES has been replaced by other cancer-causing growth stimulants which, for all practical purposes, are impossible to monitor in the meat supply.

— Chlordane was used for years in our homes to kill termites. Velsicol Chemical, which makes it, withheld reports showing it caused cancer in animals.

— Ignoring reports that the weed-killing chemical molinate causes harm to men's reproductive systems, California approved the continued use of the herbicide in rice fields.

fish, which store PCBs in their fat (PCBs are apparently carried north by the wind and absorbed by algae, plankton, cod, and then marine mammals). Women in industrialized countries commonly have dioxins and furans—chlorine-containing by-products of chemical manufacturing and waste incineration—in their breast milk.

The Great Unknown

People are now exposed to thousands more chemicals than were their ancestors of a mere 150 years ago, but the world's understanding of how all these substances affect human beings is still elementary. A few years ago, the National Research

— Two scientists responsible for establishing "safe limits" for fifty-two chemicals in the workplace worked for Dow and Du Pont. Many of the chemicals were also manufactured by Dow and Du Pont.

— Monsanto's medical director, while being cross-examined in a toxic chemical-related lawsuit, conceded under oath that researchers who conducted an important Monsanto cancer death study in 1983 knowingly fudged the data to equalize the death rates in "exposed" and "unexposed" workers. This suspect study was used by industry for years to trivialize risks associated with dioxins.

— Many commercial brands of cosmetics and personal care products contain the chemicals diethanolamine and triethanolamine, also abbreviated DEA & TEA & often shown on a label attached with other ingredients, as in "Cocamide-DEA", or "TEA-sodium lauryl sulfate." Both DEA & TEA interact with other chemicals in products, while in stores, or medicine cabinets, to form cancer-causing chemicals called nitrosamines.

— Millions of American children wore nightclothes treated with the fire retardant Tris, a powerful cancer-causing agent. It required some two years before the government acted to ban the chemical. Thousands of children are likely to contact cancer as a result. U.S. manufacturers were allowed to dump Tris-treated sleepwear on the international market.

Source: "Living Healthy in a Toxic World", p149 David Steinman and R.Michael Wisner, 1996.

Council (NRC) looked into just how much is known. It found that there is no information at all on the possible toxic effects of 80 percent of the 50,000 or so industrial chemicals (a category excluding pesticides, food additives, cosmetics, and drugs) used in the United States. And there are still many important unanswered questions about the remaining 20 percent. For chemicals produced in amounts exceeding 1 million pounds a year, for example, the council found that no testing had been done to determine whether there is potential for neurobehavioral damage, birth defects, or other toxic effects that might be passed on through several generations.

Though chemical manufacturers usually don't submit full reports on their product's potential toxic effects, independent researchers have documented some of them. Based on current scientific literature, the NRC estimates that one-third of the 197 substances to which a million or more American workers are exposed have the potential to be neurotoxic, which means they can damage the central nervous system and the brain. A partial list of these products includes many solvents, pesticides, and several metals.

Many common industrial substances including benzene, dioxin, certain pesticides, and some metals also have the ability to interfere with the immune system,.Many organochlorines, including DDT, dioxins, furans and PCBs, as well as the pesticides chlordane, heptachlor, and hexachlorobenzene, disrupt the endocrine system and impair reproductive abilities.While some toxic organochlorine substances have been banned in the United States and other countries, they can persist in the environment for decades, and many, like DDT, are still used in other parts of the world. Shoe polish, glues, household cleaners, varnishes, and other everyday consumer products stored in the home contain

Box 9.2. COTTON, PESTICIDES AND SUICIDES

India — Death has walked through the village and the dying crop whispers a dirge for the body of Kaselte Sammiah, a poor cotton farmer who committed suicide in the village of Sitarampur in Andhra Pradesh. Sammiah died February 1, 1998 after consuming one half liter of Moncrotophos, a pesticide that failed to protect his cotton crop. He is survived by seven children.

Since June 1997, at least 80 farmers have committed suicide in the state. On February 3, Mutyalapali Subbaiah, a farmer from the district of Prakasam, attempted to commit suicide in front of a public official at a rally in Markapur.

"Since the beginning of the new year, not a single day has passed without one cotton farmer committing suicide", says a farmer in Warangal, where almost the entire standing cotton crop had been devastated, placing communities on the brink of starvation.

Faced with a raging attack on the cotton crop by Spodoptera litura (tobacco cutworm), frantic Andhra Pradesh farmers were sitting ducks for pesticide suppliers offering to sell pesticides on credit. But the indiscriminate application of pesticides only led to increased resistance in pests. While pests continued to ravage crops, expenses mounted and the noose tightened. What followed was a spate of suicides.

Despite the efforts of national and state agricultural research institutions, losses from pests were ranging from 10 to 30 percent, according to officials with the Indian Council of Agriculture Research (ICAR). On January 7, the government decided that loss of crops constituted a "national calamity" and began extending debt relief to farmers—a humiliating acceptance of the failure of crop science.

Desperate farmers used pesticides in quantities that astounded even pesticide dealers, who reaped a rich harvest with sales of methomyl and other highly poisonous pesticides.

The powerful pesticide lobby was one of the chief promoters of the switch from sustainable, low-yielding traditional cultivators to cash crops like cotton because they are susceptible to a host of pests and require frequent application of pesticides.

Source : Earth Island Journal, p 29, Jitedra Verma Fall 1998.

neurotoxic chemicals. Some hazardous waste sites harbor neurotoxic chemicals that threaten the drinking supplies in nearby communities.

But little is known about the precise extent to which people are exposed outside the workplace to a given toxic chemical, let alone about the variety of hazardous substances in the environment. Experts are also unsure, in many cases, how much—or little—of an exposure will produce subtle adverse effects in people. As a result, it is difficult to assess how likely it is that a majority of people may be suffering from exposure to a wide range of industrial substances.

Lead Weight

In the 1970s, the U.S. government banned the use of lead in gasoline and household paint. Two decades later, government officials estimate that one of every six children in the U.S. under the age of five has enough lead in her blood to be at risk for health consequences.

Although lead persists as a health problem in the U.S., the United States government and the American medical establishment are still far ahead of the rest of the world in understanding and combating its effects. "Many countries in Europe have not yet reached the conclusion that lead is as much a hazard as it is seen to be in the United States", says Polly Hoppin, a senior program officer for pollution prevention at the World Wildlife Fund. Nonetheless, lead is a huge environmental health threat in many European countries as well as a growing menace in India, Mexico, Thailand and many other developing countries.

An ubiquitous metal that is part of many different manufacturing processes, lead is still used even in the United States in batteries, fishing weights, ammunition, solder, ceramic glaze, aprons used by radiation workers and in paint applied to bridges and the hulls of ships. Lead from waste dumps, air borne dust, peeling paint and other sources settles into the soil as well. Despite the U.S. ban of lead-based household paint in 1978, the main source of lead "pollution" is still lead house paint, 3 million tons of old lead line the walls and homes of 57 million American homes and 74 percent of all private housing built before 1980 contains some lead paint, according to the U.S. Department of Health and Human Services.

Lead can create IQ deficits of up to eight points in children, according to some studies, without any outward, recognizable signs of damage. Although people have recognized lead's toxic properties for 2,000 years, appreciation of the subtle damage wrought by low-level exposure is very recent. U.S. government agencies, such as EPA, the Centers for Disease Control and Prevention (CDC) and the Public Health Service, have lowered "acceptable" levels of exposure to lead by 75% since the 1970s. The CDC's new threshold for lead levels is 10 micrograms per deciliter of blood. Anything higher is likely to impair intellectual development.

Beyond nervous system damage, lead exposure may also impair fertility, cause menstrual disorders and induce anemia, high blood pressure and kidney problems. But these effects occur mostly among workers in industries that use lead, according to Ellen Silbergeld, an Epidemiologist at the University of Maryland's School of Medicine in Baltimore. Lead may also dampen immune responses, though research on this aspect of its toxicity has yielded conflicting results. Unfortunately, in lead-polluted countries that have yet to recognize the substance's dangers, children remain at a great risk of being robbed of their intellectual potential.

Hormonally Driven

While the dioxin story is less flashed out than the lead saga, dioxin may prove to have more effects on the human body. Outside the workplace, lead primarily threatens the central nervous system, but dioxin, an industrial by-product, appears capable of interfering with a number of physiological systems.

Dioxin is created by the paper industry's chlorine bleaching, by waste incineration and as an unintended by-product of the manufacture of dacthal, a pesticide and pentachlorophenol, a wood preservative. However, no one has been able to account for the sources of up to half the dioxin in the environment.

More than 90 percent of exposure to dioxin comes from food, particularly meat, dairy products and fish. While dioxin commonly refers to a particular compound known as tetrachlorodibenzo-p-dioxin, or TCDD, there are actually 75 different dioxins. TCDD, the substance found in Agent Orange, a defoliant used widely during the Vietnam War, is the most toxic dioxin. Researchers now think that low-level exposure to dioxin damages the immune system and reproductive functions. Dioxin also appears to affect behavior and learning ability, which suggests that it is neurotoxic. As with lead, researchers have found that dioxin is most damaging to very young animals, especially those that are exposed while in the uterus.

In the 1980s, dioxin was widely believed to be the most potent animal carcinogen ever known. More recently, though, intense controversy has cropped up over the true nature of dioxin's toxicity in people. To resolve conflicting claims about dioxin's potency, EPA embarked in 1993 on an in-depth study. Instead of focusing just on cancer, the agency decided to examine all of dioxin's potential toxic effects—including those involving metabolism, behavior, the immune system, reproduction and development of the fetus. This study is now raising concern in the minds of toxicologists over dioxin's potential effects on human reproductive & immune systems. Recent studies have found higher rates of certain kinds of cancer among workers exposed to dioxin. But if reproductive and immune system damage occurs at much lower levels of exposure than those associated with cancer, far more people may be at risk for these subtle effects.

Normal development and reproductive abilities in animals are apparently affected by dioxin when the chemical interferes by amplifying or diminishing the effect of natural sexual hormones at a critical point during pregnancy. Depending on whether it produces estrogen or testosterone, the fetus develops "female" or "male" features. Later in life, hormones direct sexual behavior and regulate fertility. "The slightest shift of the ratio of male hormones to female hormones will alter development irrevocably", says the World Wildlife Fund's Theo Colborn.

Despite new research by EPA scientists and others, many questions remain about dioxin, not to mention the thousands of other chemicals that have never been studied.

Human Guinea Pigs

Scientists despair of the void in research on toxic chemicals, but there are plenty of experiments in progress around the world. Most of us are involuntary research subjects, exposed to not just one, but a wide variety of chemicals every day, some of which remain in our bodies for months or even years. (Dioxin lingers in the body for more than a decade). If scientists know little about the effects of individual chemicals on the body, they are certainly ill equipped to evaluate the combined toxicity of multiple chemicals. One study by the National Institute of Environmental Health Sciences compared the effect on mice's immune response of a mixture of 25 chemicals commonly found in U.S. groundwater with the effects of individual chemicals. The researchers concluded that the potency of the 25-chemical mixture was greater than the individual strength of any one chemical. "Put the paper industry on a chlorine-free diet and you will get rid of a lot of dioxin", says Tom Webster, a bioligist at the City University of New York (CUNY).

The EPA's reassessment of dioxin will provide a model for future studies of toxic chemicals' subtle effects on both adults and children and may very well be worth its $3 to $4 million cost. On the other hand, is it fair to continue making people the unwitting guinea pigs in industries' quest for better, faster manufacturing and products? Shouldn't the burden of safety be placed squarely upon industry?

The philosopher Hannah Arendt once observed that it is the nature of evil to make itself appear unremarkable and common-place. Likewise, chemicals now occupy such a comfortable niche in our lives that we fail to consider their dual nature. The time may have come to hold these life-changing substances to a far stricter standard and consider them guilty until proven innocent.

....

The Rivet Poppers

Paul & Anne Ehrlich

*Build then the ship of death, for you must take the longest
journey to oblivion.*
— *D. H. Lawrence*

As you walk from the terminal toward your airliner, you notice
a man on a ladder busily prying rivets out of its wing. Somewhat
concerned, you saunter over to the rivet popper and ask him just
what the hell he's doing.

"I work for the airline—Growthmania Intercontinental," the
man informs you, "and the airline has discovered that it can sell
these rivets for two dollars apiece." "But how do you know you
won't fatally weaken the wing doing that?" you inquire.

"Don't worry," he assures you. "I'm certain the manufacturer
made this plane much stronger than it needs to be, so no harm's
done. Besides, I've taken lots of rivets from this wing and it hasn't
fallen off yet. Growthmania Airlines needs the money; if we
didn't pop the rivets, Growthmania wouldn't be able to continue
expanding. And I need the commission they pay me—fifty cents
a rivet!"

"You must be out of your mind!"

"I told you not to worry; I know what I'm doing. As a matter
of fact, I'm going to fly on this flight also, so you can see there's
absolutely nothing to be concerned about."

Any sane person would, of course, go back into the terminal,
report the gibbering idiot and Growthmania Airlines to the FAA,
and make reservations on another carrier. You never have to fly
on an airliner. But unfortunately all of us are passengers on a
very large spacecraft—one on which we have no option but to

fly. And, frighteningly, it is swarming with rivet poppers behaving in ways analogous to that just described.

The rivet poppers on Spaceship Earth include such people as the President of the United States, the Chairman of the Soviet Communist Party, and most other politicians and decision makers; many big businessmen and small businessmen; and, inadvertently, most other people on the planet, including you and us. Philip Handler, the president of the United States National Academy of Sciences, is an important rivet popper, and so are industrialist Daniel Ludwig (who is energetically chopping down the Amazon rainforest), Senator Howard Baker, enemy of the Snail Darter, and Vice-President George Bush, friend of nuclear war. Others prominent on the rivet-popper roster include Japanese whalers and woodchippers, many utility executives, the auto moguls of Detroit, the folks who run the AMAX corporation, almost all economists, the Brazilian government, Secretary of the Interior James Watt, the Editors of Science, Scientific American, and the Wall Street Journal, the bosses of the pesticide industry, some of the top bureaucrats of the U.S. Department of Agriculture and some of those in the Department of the Interior, the officers of the Entomological Society of America, the faculties of every engineering school in the world, the Army Corps of Engineers, and the hierarchy of the Roman Catholic Church.

Now all of these people (and especially you and we) are certainly not crazy or malign. Most of them are in fact simply uninformed—which is one reason for writing an article on the processes and consequences of rivet-popping.

Rivet-popping on Spaceship Earth consists of aiding and abetting the extermination of species and populations of nonhuman organisms. The European Lion, the Passenger Pigeon, the Carolina Parakeet, and the Sthenele Brown Butterfly are some of the numerous rivets that are now irretrievably gone; the

Chimpanzee, Mountain Gorilla, Siberian Tiger, Right Whale, and California Condor are prominent among the many rivets that are already loosened. The rest of the perhaps ten million species and billions of distinct populations still more or less hold firm. Some of these species supply or could supply important direct benefits to humanity, and all of them are involved in providing free public services without which society could not persist.

The natural ecological systems of Earth, which supply these vital services, are analogous to the parts of an airplane that make it a suitable vehicle for human beings. But ecosystems are much more complex than wings or engines. Ecosystems, like well-made airplanes, tend to have redundant subsystems and other "design" features that permit them to continue functioning after absorbing a certain amount of abuse. A dozen rivets, or a dozen species, might never be missed. On the other hand, a thirteenth rivet popped from a wing flap, or the extinction of a key species involved in the cycling of nitrogen, could lead to a serious accident.

In most cases an ecologist can no more predict the consequences of the extinction of a given species than an airline passenger can assess the loss of a single rivet. But both can easily foresee the long-term results of continually forcing species to extinction or of removing rivet after rivet. No sensible airline passenger today would accept a continuous loss of rivets from jet transports. Before much more time has passed, attitudes must be changed so that no sane passenger on Spaceship Earth will accept a continuous loss of populations or species of nonhuman organisms.

Over most of the several billion years during which life has flourished on this planet, its ecological systems have been under what would be described by the airline industry as "progressive maintenance." Rivets have dropped out or gradually worn out, but they were continuously being replaced; in fact, over much of the time our spacecraft was being strengthened by the insertion of more rivets than were being lost. Only since about ten thousand years ago has there been any sign that that process might be more or less permanently reversed. That was when a single species, Homo sapiens, began its meteoric rise to planetary dominance. And only in about the last half-century has it become clear that humanity has been forcing species and populations to extinction at a rate greatly exceeding that of natural attrition and far beyond the rate at which natural processes can replace them. In the last twenty-five years or so, the disparity between the rate of loss and the rate of replacement has become alarming; in the next twenty-five years, unless something is done, it promises to become catastrophic for humanity.

The form of the catastrophe is, unfortunately, difficult to predict. Perhaps the most likely event will be an end of civilization as in T.S. Eliot's whimper. As nature is progressively impoverished, its ability to provide a moderate climate, cleanse air and water, recycle wastes, protect crops from pests, replenish soil, and so on, will be increasingly degraded. The human population

---

Box 10.1. THE TIGER

From earliest artistic efforts on dark cave walls, human societies have celebrated the tiger. The fear, awe, and wonder inspired by this largest of all cats resonate in diverse forms down through the centuries, from ancient carvings of the Indus Valley and the 18th-century poetry of William Blake to modern-day children's stories and trucks decorated with images of the Hindu deity Durga astride a tiger.

The tiger's symbolic weight has not prevented people from killing it as a threat to life and property, hunting it for sport and trophies, and destroying its habitat. Instead, the tiger's legendary strength actually contributes to its destruction. Some Asian cultures imbue the tiger with enormous healing powers and use various tiger parts–especially bone, but also hair, teeth, skin, and many other parts–as cures for dozens of ailments. Across their historic range, from the Russian Far East to the southern tip

will be growing as the capacity of Earth to support people is shrinking. Rising death rates and a falling quality of life will lead to a crumbling of post-industrial civilization. The end may come so gradually that the hour of its arrival may not be recognizable, but the familiar world of today will disappear within the life span of many people now alive.

Of course, the "bang" is always possible. For example, it is likely that destruction of the rich complex of species in the Amazon basin would trigger rapid changes in global climatic patterns. Agriculture remains heavily dependent on stable climate, and human beings remain dependent on food. By the end of the century the extinction of perhaps a million species in the Amazon basin could have entrained famines in which a billion human beings perished. And if our species is very unlucky, the famines could lead to a thermonuclear war, which could extinguish civilization.

Fortunately, the accelerating rate of extinctions can be arrested. It will not be easy; it will require both the education of, and concerted action by, hundreds of millions of people.

of Sumatra, tigers now face extinction in the wild. Tigers living around the Caspian Sea went extinct in the last century. Populations of tigers that once roamed the islands of Java and Bali are now extinct. Threats to the survival of healthy wild tiger populations include rampant poaching, spurred by the Oriental medicinal trade; over-hunting of the tiger's prey; and unabated habitat loss from fragmentation and conversion to other land uses.

Tigers also play a key role in conservation, for they are "umbrella" species—species requiring such large areas of habitat that conserving them also conserves vast intact wild areas that support thousands of other species of mammals, birds, amphibians, reptiles, fish, and insects.

Saving the tiger requires mobilizing a global conservation effort that addresses all the threats facing the species, including habitat degradation, poaching, illeagal trade, and human pressures.

But no tasks are more important, because extinctions of other organisms must be stopped before the living structure of our spacecraft is so weakened that at a moment of stress it fails and civilization is destroyed.

....

Serene, I fold my hands, and wait,
Nor care for wind, nor tide, nor sea;
I have no more 'gainst time or fate,
For lo! my own shall come to me.

— *'Waiting', John Burroughs.*

How we learn about our Home

*" I prefer the company of peasants because they have
not been educated sufficiently to reason incorrectly."*

— *Michel de Montaigne*

Of Learning and Immortality

Then they asked:
"Master, what is education?"
The wise man spoke silently,
"There is no master
and no education,
my people."
People were bemused;
Master continued:
"Life is an opportunity
to realize ourselves.
We are the creatures
of learning.
To learn is to be creative.
To learn is to know
the root of our existence.
To learn is to preserve
Our sacred Earth.
To learn is to live
in harmony with the whole.
To learn is to give
birth to future.
To learn is to reach
enlightenment — Nirvana.
To learn is to be
liberated
from the finiteness
of Space and Time.
To learn is to be
Immortal".
Master was no more.

— Rashmi Mayur

Education for the Future

David Hicks

We won't have a society if we destroy the environment
— Margaret Mead

The children we teach in school now will spend most of their lives in the 21st century. Those leaving school in the 1990s will become the parents, voters, workers, business people and visionaries of tomorrow. From this generation will come the leaders of the decades of the new century. When and where in the education of young people do we help them look at the kind of future they want for themselves, for society and the planet? What Toffler wrote twenty years ago still holds true today :

"All education springs from images of the future and all education creates images of the future. Thus all education, whether so intended or not, is a preparation for the future. Unless we understand the future for which we are preparing we may do tragic damage to those we teach."

Forward-looking thinking

The main purpose of this essay therefore is to provide an educational context and practical support for teachers who wish to make such a concern for the future more explicit in their classroom practice. It is based on the notion that developing skills of forward-looking thinking is vital in times of rapid change and an essential pre-requisite for responsible citizenship.

In particular, the activities in the classroom should be designed to help pupils:

— Develop a more future-orientated perspective on their own lives and events in the wider world.

— Identify and envision alternative futures which are more just and sustainable.

— Exercise their critical thinking skills and creative imagination more effectively.
— Participate in more thoughtful and informed decision-making in the present.
— Engage in active and responsible citizenship in the local and global community, on behalf of present and future generations.

This article is intended for all those people—teachers, parents, heads, governors and others who believe that young people should be encouraged to explore their hopes and fears for the future of society and the planet. It is hoped that using this book will make the National Curriculum more fun and help you sleep better at night!

Children's interests

"My hopes for the future are to have a happy life and to live for a long time and have a nice family. And that my cat and goldfish will live for a long time..."

"I hope that in the future there will be no more war and hunger and the world will become green and everybody will unite again."

"Another world fear is that the atmosphere will get too polluted so that we cannot live any longer."

These are the concerns of some 10-year olds from a Berkshire school. They range from the personal to the global, from their families and pets to the welfare of other people and the planet itself. Should we educate young people to accept unthinkingly the status quo or should we encourage them to reflect critically on the world in order to improve it? What does effective preparation for the 21st century look like in a multicultural society and an interdependent world?

Research from the Henley Center for Forecasting shows that young people in school are very aware of, and concerned about, global issues. In particular they see the environment as a key concern, with destruction of the ozone layer, deforestation, global warming, CFCs and endangered species as the problems most urgently requiring attention. Next they cite more local problems such as factory and chemical pollution, pollution of rivers and seas, and car emissions. Generally children show a high level of interest in environmental issues, with school lessons and projects being cited as their main source of information. However, over 60 % of the children surveyed still said they didn't think enough was taught about the environment at school.

It is natural that children should be concerned both about the current state of the planet and also the future. They are aware that many global issues, and not only environmental ones affect their lives now and that the future holds both promise and threat. For children, the future is everything since most of their lives are still ahead of them.

As the children well know, their future adult life will be greatly affected by what is happening in the world today. It is important therefore, for teachers and pupils to develop some critical sense of the current state of the world (where we are now) and also of future possibilities (where we want to get to).

Alternative futures

The end of one century and the beginning of another always acts as a question mark for society. Thus during the 1990s attention is increasingly being drawn to the future. What do we want to leave behind and want to take with us? Where are we going and does this bear any relation to where we'd like to go? What does a better world look like? And for whom would it be better? If we are to avoid a curriculum that is merely nationalistic, such questions must always begin with the current state of the planet, both in our communities and globally.

Box 11.1. **COMPUTER-AIDED ENVIRONMENTAL EDUCATION:
PROBLEMS AND PROMISES**

Computer-aided environmental education, the utilization of computer technology to promote the goals and objectives of environmental education, has recently passed through an era of adolescence—a time full of contradictions and mistakes born of inexperience. Today, while still in the early stages of development, computer-aided environmental education is moving forward with a new sophistication and depth. Given the progress to date and the possibilities for the very near future, computer-aided environmental education may prove to be our most powerful educational tool for promoting everything from environmental awareness to environmental action.

Problems

— Following the introduction of any new technological tool there is almost always a period of euphoria. Unfortunately, that euphoria soon fades as unrealistic expectations go unfounded, associated costs are discovered, and resistance to change is encountered. In our zeal to apply computer-aided instruction and communication to promote environmental education, there have certainly been examples of "trying to fit a square peg into a round hole." We need to remind ourselves that we don't have to use the technology just because it exists. Just because it's on a floppy disk doesn't mean it's necessarily worth our time and attention.

The best computer-aided environmental education is achieved when we do not allow the misapplication or inherent limits of computer technology to compromise what we know about how people think and learn.

— The utilization of computers in support of education raises several important questions of equity. Who gets access to computers? What are the monetary costs associated with computer-aided educational tools? In light of those costs, who can afford to participate? Unless both the hardware and software are kept at reasonably low-cost, the utilization of computers will only be affordable to a few. The result could be an increasing gap in the quality of educational services accessible to learning populations of different economic status.

In order for computer-aided environmental education to be effective, it must also be affordable and accessible to all.

— Why gather first-hand data on climate or water quality when you can get it through an on-line database? Why go bird watching when you can access a videodisc of 50,000 color slides of birds, cross referenced and selected at the push of a button? Computer-aided environmental education has positive potential only when used as a catalyst, and never as a substitute, for field based instruction or exploration.

— It can be argued that computers are used in a variety of ways to benefit the environment. Because telecommunications can increase communication between geographically distant individuals, it can help to reduce the need for regular face-to-face meetings, thereby saving the fossil fuel used in transportation. On the other hand, numerous negative environmental impacts are byproducts of computer utilization. The production of high technology components makes use of toxic gases, solvents, heavy metals and volatile organic compounds that can adversely impact workers, communities and the environment. Huge amounts of contaminated waste by-products are generated and must be handled and disposed of properly. In addition, the high tech industry is probably the world's largest single source of chlorofluorocarbons. Add to this the increased electrical demand from computers, printers, and monitors. Throw in the reams of paper used by computing and you've got a considerable set of waste and pollution problems associated with computer-aided EE.

Computer-aided environmental education must be held to the same environmental impact assessment we would give any technology. Only judicious use can result in a positive net impact on the biophysical environment.

Promises of Computer Aided Environmental Education:

In spite of the fundamental problems outlined above, computer-aided environmental education presents a whole new set of extremely powerful tools for promoting, as perhaps never before, the goals and objectives of environmental education.

1. Environmental Hypermedia, Videodiscs and CD-ROM

Hypermedia (sometimes know as "interactive multimedia") combines several instructional technologies to form an extraordinarily powerful medium. Color video images, sound, text and searchable data all come together in a multisensory, highly dynamic learning frontier. At the heart of this medium is the laser videodisc, an inexpensive, easy-to-use visual storage and retrieval technology. Vast amounts of audio and visual information can be stored on a single laser videodisc, thereby creating a visual database. As many as 54,000 images can be stored on each side of a 12-inch disc and these images can be programmed in any combination— slides, graphics and motion clips. For comparison, a two-sided laser videodisc has the information equivalent of 5,000 double-density floppy diskettes!

2. Environmental Simulation/Modeling

Simulation and modeling programs can demonstrate in a visual, dynamic format, the complex interaction of environmental systems as well as the impacts of human activity. Computers allow us, as never before, to simulate complex systems and to investigate the implications of our actions before we initiate them.

3. Interactive Environmental Software

Instructional software has made some major advances in the last few years. A new generation of graphic, interactive environmental software programs now enable self-paced, learner-contoured environmental investigation and education.

Animation, sound, color and pictures now enliven a software world which was previously occupied almost exclusively by words and numbers. A whole new generation of "authoring programs" (such as Hypercard and Course of Action) can also be added to this more sophisticated approach to environmental computer software.

4. Environmental Distance Learning & Telecommunications

Low-cost telecommunication tools allow us to dialogue and cooperate directly with students and educators around the world (or across your bioregion). Using readily available technologies, in a matter of seconds we can send and receive information from around the planet— thereby shrinking the planet in time and space to the scale of a "global village."

Our students, for example, can search comprehensive environmental databases or instantaneously share field data and correspond with other classrooms across the nation or across the oceans. Whether you're a teacher, a student, a resource specialist, or an advocate, the environmental distance learning opportunities made available by today's telecommunications technologies exhibit tremendous potential.

We can dismiss computer-aided environmental education because of the problems outlined above or we can explore, with care and creativity, how these new technological tools can be coupled with what we already know about effective environmental education.

Source : "Computer-Aided Environmental Education", edited by W.J. Rocky Rohwedder, 1990.

State of the world

Lester Brown, Director of the Worldwatch institute, writes: "As the nineties begin, the world is on the edge of a new age ...we are now at one of those rare points in history – a time of great change, a time when change is as unpredictable as it is inevitable. No one can say with certainty what the new world will look like. But if we are to fashion a promising future for the next generation, then the enormous effort required to reverse the environmental degradation of the planet will dominate world affairs for decades to come.."

Problems of inequality, injustice, environmental damage, violence and war are present in our own society and communities as well as on a global scale, it is increasingly recognized that they cannot be seen as separate problems. They are, rather, part of a single global crisis, involving our economy, technology, welfare, environment and ways of relating to each other. It is in this crisis and our attempts to resolve it, which will drastically affect the lives of future generations.

Novel teaching skills for global issues

There is a long history in the UK of innovative teaching about such issues. Two frameworks which, help 'make sense of the world' include those relating to gender relationships and global economics. They each provide a useful lens as it were through which to study the problems of everyday life.

Archaeological evidence indicates that up until 5000 years ago, a partnership model of society predominated, with a flourishing of the arts and crafts and a high valuation of nature. Then followed a long period of social upheaval in which the dominator model, with its stress on male dominance, hierarchy, violence against women, and exploitation of the environment, came to be accepted as the norm.

Eisler argues that none of this is inevitable, that we can rediscover the partnership ethic and not repeat the mistakes of the past in the future. The emergence of a strong women's movement and environmental movement over the last two decades suggests that very different directions for the future are indeed available to us now.

A second framework for making sense of the world focuses on economic inequality.

"Today, commodity chains criss-cross the globe, linking producers of raw materials with processors, manufacturers and consumers. Consumption in one society depends on production in another far away, and consumers generally remain unaware of the social and environmental impacts of what they consume. The world economy is one based on profit and the accumulation of capital; a process which can only take place through unequal exchange and the exploitation of people and environments throughout the world."

This viewpoint argues that the majority of people in Western Europe, the USA and Japan enjoy a high standard of living as a result of the continuing process of unequal exchange with the countries of the South. Much of the trade, aid and investment given, far from helping overcome poverty, enmeshes them even more in the economic and political policies of the North. As Gandhi commented, there is enough for everyone's need on this planet, but not for everyone's greed.

The origins of the present global crisis thus lie in both the assumptions we hold and the structures we have created for managing economics, society and the environment. One way of challenging these structures and assumptions is by asking questions about what sort of future we want.

Envisioning the future

The approach of the third millennium will concentrate people's mind on the future. The year 2000 or 2001 to be exact, acts as a symbolic threshold, a metaphor for the future itself. A last decade turns into a first, one century turns into another, the second millennium into the third. It presents us with an opportunity to reexamine ourselves, our values and institutions, how we feel about the world we have inherited and what sort of world we wish to create. Educators have a crucial role to play in asking such critical questions about the future.

The images that we have of the future matter because they help determine our priorities in the present. Such images play a critical role in the creation of change. They exert a powerful influence over what people think is, or is not, worth doing in the present. It is important to recall that there is no such thing as the future (singular), for at any given moment in time any number of futures (plural) are actually possible. The term 'alternative futures' is thus used as a shorthand reminder of this.

For any exploration of alternative futures to be of use it also needs to be remembered that different people and different groups have quite different views of the future. Consider the different perspectives that a child in London, a single parent in Wales, a worker in Dresden or a mother in Brazil, might have. Clearly some groups in society have much more power than others to define the future, generally those who are rich in the global system or who wield power through, say transnational corporations, international banking, governments, the military, the media. In some sense such groups also colonize the future, particularly big business with its constant creation of new 'needs' for tomorrow.

Every culture has its dream, whether religious or secular, of a past or future better world. In Western thought this aspiration has become known as utopia. Utopias are blueprints for a better future society and utopians may present their ideas as fiction, where the ideal society is set in some other time or place or as a program for political action and change.

Clearly utopias reflect the age in which they are conceived but they always have a double-edged message: a critique of present imperfections and a vision of a better world. Literary utopias range from Plato's *Republic* and Thomas More's *Utopia* to William Morris's famous *News from Nowhere* and Marge Piercy's *Woman on the Edge of Time*. Stephen Coleman writes: "The utopian imagination, at its most radical, invades the prevailing concept of reality, undermines certainties about what humans must always be like, and casts doubt upon the inevitabilities of the relations of everyday life". This longstanding and vital tradition can continue to inspire critical action for change and nourish our creative imagination today.

A Sustainable Society : A way forward.

The most essential element in any notion of a preferable future must be that of sustainable development, a major focus of concern at the Earth Summit in 1992. Indeed it has been argued that education about the need for such development should be an integral part of education in all countries.

Traditional models of development and ideas of progress generally, narrowly focus on economic growth (GNP as a measure of consumption) with its intrinsic discounting of other 'costs'. Thus some people benefit at the expense of others; people benefit at the expense of the environment; and people today benefit at the expense of future generations.

In contrast, sustainable development emphasizes increased levels of social and economic well-being, particularly for the least advantaged; increased emphasis on the protection of the biosphere on which all life depends; and that future generations should inherit at least as much wealth, natural and person-made, as we ourselves inherited.

Working towards a sustainable future requires production planned to meet human needs together with a more just distribution of resources. It means reducing the harmful effects of industry and new technology, challenging company policies which are dangerous to people and the environment, stopping aid programs which are inappropriate and damaging, reducing over-consumption and waste, restraining population growth, distinguishing clearly between wants and needs, and organising locally, nationally and internationally for appropriate change.

To understand that there is not one single future but various possible futures, highlights the need to make choices between alternatives. The current state of the planet requires that exploration of just and sustainable futures becomes a major priority at all levels of education in society. Future generations would surely ask no less of us than this.

....

The Sense of Wonder

Rachel Carson

The most beautiful thing we can experience is the mysterious.
It is the source of all true art and science.

— *Albert Einstein*

One stormy night when my nephew Roger was about 20 months old, I wrapped him in a blanket and carried him down to the beach in the rainy darkness. Out there, just at the edge of where-we-couldn't-see, big waves were thundering in, dimly seen white shapes that boomed and shouted and threw great handfuls of froth at us. Together we laughed for pure joy – he, a baby meeting for the first time the wild tumult of Oceanus. I, with the salt of half a lifetime of sea love in me. But I think we felt the same spine-tingling response to the vast, roaring ocean and the wild night around us.

A night or two later the storm had blown itself out and I took Roger again to the beach, this time to carry him along the waters' edge, piercing the darkness with the yellow cone of our flashlight. Our adventure on this particular night had to do with life, for we were searching for ghost crabs, those sand-coloured fleet legged beings which Roger had sometimes glimpsed briefly on the beaches in daytime. But the crabs are chiefly nocturnal and when not roaming the night beaches, they dig little pits near the surf line, where they hide, seemingly watching and waiting for what the sea may bring them. For me, the sight of these small living creatures, solitary and fragile against the brute force of the sea, had moving philosophic overtones, and I do not pretend that Roger and I reacted with similar emotions. But it was good to see his infant acceptance of a world of elemental things, fearing neither the song of the wind nor the darkness nor the roaring surf, entering with baby excitement into the search for a "ghos". . . .

We are continuing that sharing of adventures in the world of nature that we began in his babyhood, and I think the results are good. The sharing includes nature in storm as well as calm, by night as well as day, and is based on having fun together rather than on teaching.

When Roger has visited me in Maine and we have walked in these woods, I have made no conscious effort to name plants or animals nor to explain to him, but have just expressed my own pleasure in what we see, calling his attention to this or that but only as I would share discoveries with an older person. Later I have been amazed at the way names stick in his mind, for when I show color slides of my wood-plants, it is Roger who can identify them "Oh! That is what Rachael likes, that is bunch-berry!" Or " that is Juniper, but you can't eat those green berries – they are for the squirrels". I am sure no amount of drill would have implanted the names so firmly as just going through the woods in the spirit of two friends on an expedition of exciting discovery.

We have let Roger share our enjoyment of things people ordinarily deny children because they are inconvenient, interfering with bedtime, or involving wet clothing that has to be changed or mud that has to be cleaned off the rug. We have let him join us in the dark living room before the big picture window to watch the full moon riding lower and lower toward the far shore as the light strikes the flakes of mica embedded in them.

I think we have felt that the memory of such a scene, photographed year after year by his child's mind, would mean more to him in manhood than the sleep he was losing. He told me, it would, in his own way, when we had a full moon, the night after his arrival last summer. He sat quietly on my lap for sometime, watching the moon and the water and all the night sky, and then he whispered, "I'm glad we came".

A child's world is fresh and new and beautiful, full of wonder and excitement. It is our misfortune that for most of us that clear-eyed vision, that true instinct for what is beautiful and awe inspiring is dimmed and even lost before we reach adulthood. If I had influence with the good fairy who is supposed to preside over the christening of all children I should ask that her gift to each child in the world be a sense of wonder so indestructible that it would last throughout life, as an unfailing antidote against the boredom and disenchantments of later years, the sterile preoccupation with things that are artificial, the alienation from the sources of our strength.

Exploring nature with your child is largely a matter of becoming receptive to what lies all around you. It is learning again to use your eyes, ears, nostrils and fingertips, opening up the disused channels of sensory impression.

For most of us, knowledge of our world comes largely through sight, yet we look about with such unseeing eyes that we are partially blind. One way to open your eyes to unnoticed beauty is to ask yourself, "What if I had never seen this before? What if I knew I would never see it again?"

I remember a summer night when such a thought came to me strongly. It was a clear night without a moon. With a friend, I went out on a flat headland that is almost a tiny island, being all but surrounded by the waters of the bay. There the horizons are remote and distant rims on the edge of space. We lay and looked up at the sky and the millions of stars that blazed in darkness. The night was so still that we could hear the buoy on the ledges out beyond the mouth of the bay. Once or twice, a word spoken by someone on the far shore was carried across on the clear air. A few lights burned in cottages. Otherwise there was no reminder of the Milky way flowing across the sky, the patterns of the constellations standing out bright and clear, a blazing planet low

Pedagogy of the Earth

on the horizon. Once or twice, a meteor burned its way into the earth's atmosphere.

It occurred to me that if this were a sight that could be seen only once in a century or even once in a human generation, this little

---

Box 12.1. **EDUCATION IN ANCIENT INDIA**

The ancient Indian system of education was naturally designed, from the earliest times to serve the ends of life – the four-fold ideal of 'purusartha'. It aimed at moulding the tender youth into an individual desirous and capable of living a full life as well as of achieving its highest goal. The individual was to be trained to realize the trivarga of 'dharma', 'artha' and 'kama' and thereby attain 'moksa'. Therefore, 'Dharma' and 'Brahma' came to be the two-fold subject matter of education. The student was initiated into a life of investigation of the nature and mystery of the Universal Order (Rta) of inquiring into the principles of social life (dharma) and of practising methods of expanding his individual personality into the Absolute. Thus, the ancient Indian system was a comprehensive scheme of perfecting the individual personality in all its facets – physical, moral, intellectual, religious and spiritual. The educated individual was expected to be a useful, enlightened citizen, fulfilling his obligations cheerfully, serving the society selflessly and thereby reaching the highest goal of Universal Harmony.

Knowledge was considered as a value for it was the source of all happiness as well as the means of realizing the highest goal. In this world there is nothing as sacred as knowledge. Without knowledge, a man is but a beast. No wonder that education and learning came to be invested with holiness. The ancient Indians developed an attitude of highest reverence towards learning and all that is associated with it. 'Jnana' itself is Brahman, Guru is god, the highest-para-brahma. The speech –'vak', through which all knowledge is attainable is divine. The intellect (dhi), without which all attempt to gain knowledge is bound to be fruitless, is again a form of divinity. The school is the very temple. To build schools, to feed the students, to patronize scholarship and to teach without any fee are some of the most sacred duties of the householders. The student is 'brahmacharin' – one who is on a pilgrimage towards the highest goal.

The most striking feature of the gurukula or school was its community life. It was basically the residence of 'guru', the teacher. He lived in a

headland would be thronged with spectators. But it can be seen many scores of nights in any year, and so the lights burned in the cottages and the inhabitants probably gave not a thought to the beauty overhead; and because they could see it almost any night

hermitage with his family. He admitted students as members of his family and provided for them free board, lodge, medical aid, education and training.

The student participated in all the activities of the household—domestic, religious, social and cultural.

Situated on the bank of a river or a lake, amidst enchanting sylvan surroundings, the 'asrama' school provided its inmates numerous opportunities of study of plants, flowers, birds and animals as well as of recreation and sport. It is not difficult to imagine the young boys and girls of the asrama gathering together in collective singing, recitation, sports, competitions and discussions. Thus, the spirit and art of corporate life were fostered.

The 'asrama' with its many scholars on its campus was undoubtedly a veritable university. The students had a wide scope for continuously widening their intellectual horizon as well as enriching their spiritual experience. The 'asramas' were, thus, great centres of advanced learning, religion and culture. No wonder, as Rabindranatha Tagore rightly remarks, 'the current of civilization that flowed from these **forest schools** inundated the whole of India'.

The ideals and aspirations of the gurukula system may be briefly summed up thus:

"That education should be free so that it would be possible for the poorer families to send their wards to the institutions for gaining knowledge."

The main aim of the Vedic educational system was to produce a rational individual, free from passions, full of universal affection, continuously self-educating and striving to reach the highest goal. His rationalism, his attitude of universal love, his entire personality had their roots in experience. His learning must reveal itself through his thought, word and deed. He must cheerfully fulfil his obligations to his family, caste, village and country. He must be emotionally alert to sacrifice his good for the good of all.

Source : Chidambra Kulkarni, 'Vedic Foundation of Indian Culture,' p 107 1973

perhaps they will never see it.

An experience like that, when one's thoughts are released to roam through the lonely spaces of the universe, can be shared with a child even if you don't know the name of a single star. You can still drink in the beauty, and think and wonder at the meaning of what you see.

....

Human beings blossom in Nature
Where the petals unfold and become
Beautiful fruits ;
Life is to be lived for love and joy.

— *Francisco Ferrer*

Knowledge in Action

" I pass with relief from the tossing sea of cause
and theory to the firm ground of result and Fact "

— *Sir Winston Spencer Churchill*

The Free Man's Worship

The life of man, viewed outwardly, is but a small thing in comparison with the forces of nature. The slave is doomed to worship Time and Fate and Death, because they are greater than anything he finds in himself, and because all his thoughts are of things which they devour. But, great as they are, to think of them greatly, to feel their passionless splendor, is greater still. And such thought makes us free men; we no longer bow before the inevitable in Oriental subjection, but we absorb it and make it a part of ourselves. To abandon the struggle for private happiness, to expel all eagerness of temporary desire, to burn with passion for eternal things—this is emancipation, and this is the free man's worship. And this liberation is effected by contemplation of Fate; for Fate itself is subdued by the mind which leaves nothing to be purged by the purifying fire of time.

Brief and powerless is man's life; on him and all his race the slow, sure doom falls pitiless and dark. Blind to good and evil, reckless of destruction, omnipotent matter rolls on its relentless way; for man, condemned today to lose his dearest, tomorrow himself to pass through the gate of darkness, it remains only to cherish, ere yet the blow fall, the lofty thoughts that ennoble his little day; disdaining the coward terrors of the slave of Fate, to worship at the shrine that his own hands have built; undismayed by the empire of chance, to preserve a mind free from the wanton tyranny that rules his outward life; proudly defiant of the irresistible forces that tolerate, for a moment, his knowledge and his condemnation, to sustain alone, a weary but unyielding Atlas, the world that his own ideals have fashioned despite the trampling march of unconscious power.

— Bertrand Russell

Ecology and Revolution

Herbert Marcuse

The great end of life is not knowledge but action
— T. H. Huxley

Coming from the United States, I am a little uneasy discussing the ecological movement, which has already by and large been co-opted (there). Among militant groups in the United States and particularly among young people, the primary commitment is to fight, with all the means (severely limited means) at their disposal, against the war crimes being committed against the Vietnamese people. The student movement—which had been proclaimed to be dead or dying, cynical and apathetic—is being re-born all over the country. This is not an organized opposition at all, but rather a spontaneous movement which organizes itself as best it can, provisionally, on the local level. But the revolt against the war in Indochina is the only oppositional movement the establishment is unable to co-opt because neocolonial war is an integral part of that global counter-revolution which is the most advanced form of monopoly capitalism.

So, why be concerned about ecology? Because the violation of the earth is a vital aspect of the counter-revolution. The genocidal war against people is also "ecocide" in so-far as it attacks the sources and resources of life itself. It is no longer enough to do away with people living now; life must also be denied to those who aren't even born yet by burning and poisoning the earth, defoliating the forests, blowing up the dikes. This bloody insanity will not alter the ultimate course of the war, but it is a very clear expression of where contemporary capitalism is at: the cruel waste of productive resources in the imperialist homeland goes hand in hand with the cruel waste of destructive forces and consumption of commodities, of death manufactured by the war industry.

In a very specific sense, the genocide and ecocide in Indochina are the capitalist response to the attempt at revolutionary ecological liberation: the bombs are meant to prevent the people of North Vietnam from undertaking the economic and social rehabilitation of the land. But in a broader sense, monopoly capitalism is waging a war against nature—human nature as well as external nature. For the demands of ever more intense exploitation come into conflict with nature itself, since nature is the source and locus of the life-instincts which struggle against the instincts of aggression and destruction. And the demands of exploitation progressively reduce and exhaust resources: the more capitalist productivity increases, the more destructive it becomes. This is one sign of the internal contradictions of capitalism.

One of the essential functions of civilization has been to change the nature of man and his natural surroundings in order to "civilize" him—that is, to make him the subject-object of the market society, subjugating the pleasure principle to the reality principle and transforming man into a tool of ever more alienated labor. This brutal and painful transformation has crept up on external nature very gradually. Certainly, nature has always been an aspect (for a long time the only one) of labor. But it was also a dimension beyond labor, a symbol of beauty, of tranquility, of a nonrepressive order. Thanks to these values, nature was the very negation of the market society, with its values of profit and utility.

However, the natural world is a historical, a social world. Nature may be a negation of aggressive and violent society, but its pacification is the work of man (and woman), the fruit of his/her productivity. But the structure of capitalist productivity is inherently expansionist: more and more, it reduces the last remaining natural space outside the world of labor and of organized and manipulated leisure.

Box 13.1. NATURE AND CAPITALISM

Advanced capitalism requires a culture which identifies the good life with consumerism. Equating the good life with material possessions is one of the few compensations left once mass society becomes the dominant way of life. With such a mass society, each person's lot is to labor at the direction of others for purposes set by others, and the only return for that labor is money, which is useful only to buy things and services. People in industrial societies have become helpless and mostly passive victims of systems that they neither understand nor control. There seems to be a developmental logic wherein industrialization leads to a mass society, which leads to passive and helpless humans. Lacking any form of transcendent meaning or a sense of being effective in public life or meaningful participation in community life, all that is left is the satisfaction available in material consumption. Industrial people literally surround themselves with concrete, which both causes and reflects a psychic and sensual numbing. The environment of daily life within which industrial people live, itself being a technological product, cannot but make nonsensical the claim that nonhuman nature itself should be respected.

The primary conclusion which follows from an examination of capitalism and socialism is that neither system holds much promise for effectively coping with ecological problems. Socialism would have the potential for far greater competence in this area if the priority of industrial production were rejected in favor of the goal of ecological sustainability. This would involve enormous changes both in the desires of people and in the social structures that are orientated toward industrial production. No societies now extant give hints at trying to do this. It is now only a theoretical prospect. One fundamental impediment to solving ecological problems is the scale of industrial societies. Mass society itself, with its tendency toward consumerism, whether capitalistic or socialistic, may be an essential part of the ecological problem.

Source : "Regarding Nature: Industrialism and deep Ecology", p 61 Andrew McLaughlin, 1993.

The process by which nature is subjected to the violence of exploitation and pollution is first of all an economic one (an aspect of the mode of production), but it is a political process as well. The power of capital is extended over the space for release and escape represented by nature. This is the totalitarian tendency of monopoly capitalism: in nature, the individual must find only a repetition of his own society; a dangerous dimension of escape and contestation must be closed off.

At the present stage of development, the absolute contradiction between social wealth and its destructive use is beginning to penetrate people's consciousnesses, even in the manipulated and indoctrinated conscious and unconscious levels of their minds. There is a feeling, a recognition, that it is no longer necessary to exist as an instrument of alienated work and leisure. There is a feeling and a recognition that well-being no longer depends on a perpetual increase in production. The revolt of youth (students, workers, and women), undertaken in the name of the values of freedom and happiness, is an attack on all the values which govern the capitalist system. And this revolt is oriented toward the pursuit of a radically different natural and technical environment; this perspective has become the basis for subversive experiments such as the attempts by American "communes" to establish non-alienated relations between the sexes, between generations, between man and nature—attempts to sustain the consciousness of refusal and of renovation

In this highly political sense, the ecological movement is attacking the "living space" of capitalism, the expansion of the realm of profit, of waste production. However, the fight against pollution is easily co-opted. Today, there is hardly an ad which doesn't exhort you to "save the environment", to put an end to pollution and poisoning. Numerous commissions are created to control the guilty parties. To be sure, the ecological movement may serve very well to spruce up the environment, to make it pleasanter, less ugly, healthier and hence, more tolerable. Obviously, this is a sort of co-optation, but it also a progressive element because, in the course of this co-optation, a certain number of needs and aspirations are beginning to be expressed

---

Box 13.2. ED ABBEY TO EARTH FIRST !

The undersigned deeply regrets that he cannot be here in the flesh—or what there is left of it. Pressing moral obligations and inescapable spiritual duties require my physical presence elsewhere—namely, floating down a river with some old cronies and a few dozen cases of beer in a godawful place called Desolation Canyon, Utah. Rejoice that you are here instead, under the blazing sun (or drenching rain) of the fairgrounds in Salt Lake City, Shithead Capital of the Inter-Mountain West. Although my feet, head, belly, etc., are out yonder, my heart is here with all of you posie-sniffers, toadstool worshippers, eco-freaks, earth-lovers, anti-nuke hardheads, environmental blowflies, FBI agents, innocent onlookers, Mothers for Peace and Winos for Ecology. You are the new salt of the Earth.

I am with you in spirit, whatever that means. And it does mean something. It means first of all that I wish to salute everyone who took part in the recent EF! road-blocking operations in the Kalmiopsis wilderness of Oregon. You are heroines and heroes and no praise for your courage, daring and irrepressible goodwill can express the admiration that we feel. I would like to name names, read the entire roll of honor, and if it were not for fear of overlooking somebody, I would do so. But you know who you are, and your pride in what you have accomplished should fill your hearts with a golden glow for the rest of your lives.

It is not enough to write letters to Congressmen, deliver sermons, make speeches, or write books. The West we love is under violent attack; the Earth that sustains us is being destroyed. Words alone will not save our country or ourselves. We need more heroes and more heroines – about a million of them. One brave deed, performed in an honorable manner and for a life-defending cause, is worth a thousand books. At some point we must draw a line across the ground of our home and our being, drive a spear into the land, and say to the bulldozers, earth-movers, government and corporations, *thus far and no farther.* If we do not we shall later feel, instead of pride, the regret of Thoreau, that good but overly-bookish man, who wrote, near the end of his life, "If I repent

within the very heart of capitalism and a change is taking place in people's behavior, experience and attitudes towards their work. Economic and technical demands are transcended in a movement of revolt which challenges the very mode of production and

to anything it is likely to be my good behavior. What demon possessed me that I behaved so well?"

We must stand up, speak out, talk back – and when necessary, fight back. The great powers ranged against us – industrial, governmental, and military – may seem omnipotent. But they are not. If enough of us resist, fiercely enough and for long enough, the huge concrete wall of the Corporate State will begin to crack. Its dams are already beginning to crack – the very bedrock beneath them is crumbling – and someday soon, if the river of the water of life continues to flow, the State's dams will go down like dominos.

Concrete and asphalt and iron are heavy, oh, so terribly massive and heavy – but water is stronger, grass is stronger. So long as the light of the sun continues to shine, the green tough grass of life will continue to grow and to break through the dead heavy static oppressive barriers of the industrial prison-house. If we are on the side of life then life is on our side. And if we are wrong we might as well get down on our knees and crawl into our little separate cells in the Beehive Society of the Technological Superstate. But we are not wrong; the grass will overcome the cement. The continuity is all.

Meanwhile, a final homily: Let's keep our bodies strong and enjoy the world. Eat more crunchy granola. Climb those mountains, run those rivers, explore those forests, investigate those deserts, love the sun and the moon and the stars and we will outlive our enemies, we will piss on their graves, and we will love and nurture and who knows—even marry their children.

Turn on, tune in, take over. Let's keep our minds, our senses and our common sense strong also. Who's in charge here? We're in charge: every man his own guru, every woman her own gurette. Who is our leader? We are all leaders. What is our program? Earth first, life first; power and profits and domination last.

Down with Empire! Up with Spring! We stand for what we stand on!

I thank you, partners.

Source : Ed Abbey, Earth first reader, edited Dave Foreman, p 247,1995 (*Originally read to a gathering of Earth Firsters !! ers that Ed was unable to attend*)

model of consumption.

Increasingly, the ecological struggle comes into conflict with the laws which govern the capitalist system: the law of increased accumulation of capital, of the creation of sufficient surplus value, of profit, of the necessity of perpetuating alienated labor and exploitation. Michel Bosquet put it very well: the ecological logic is purely and simply the negation of capitalist logic; the earth cannot be saved within the framework of capitalism, the Third World cannot be developed according to the model of capitalism.

In the last analysis, the struggle for an expansion of the world of beauty, nonviolence and serenity is a political struggle. The emphasis on these values, on the restoration of the earth as a human environment, is not just a romantic, aesthetic, poetic idea which is a matter of concern only to the privileged; today, it is a question of survival. People must learn for themselves that it is essential to change the model of production and consumption, to abandon the industry of war, waste and gadgets, replacing it with the production of those goods and services which are necessary to a life of reduced labor, of creative labor, of enjoyment.

As always, the goal is well-being, but a well-being defined not by ever-increasing consumption at the price of ever-intensified labor, but by the achievement of a life liberated from the fear, wage slavery, violence, stench and internal noise of our capitalist industrial world. The issue is not to beautify the ugliness, to conceal the poverty, to deodorize the stench, to deck the prisons, banks and factories with flowers; the issue is not the purification of the existing society but its replacement.

Pollution and poisoning are mental as well as physical phenomena, subjective as well as objective phenomena. The struggle for an environment ensuring a happier life could reinforce, in individuals themselves, the instinctual roots of their own liberation. When people are no longer capable of distinguishing between beauty and ugliness, between serenity and cacophony, they no longer understand the essential quality of freedom, of happiness. In so-far as it has become the territory of capital rather than of man, nature serves to strengthen human servitude. These conditions are rooted in the basic institutions of the established system, for which nature is primarily an object of exploitation for profit.

This is the insurmountable internal limitation of any capitalist ecology. Authentic ecology flows into a militant struggle for a socialist politics which must attack the system at its roots, both in the process of production and in the mutilated consciousness of individuals.

...

Green Politics

Carolyn Merchant

Two things fill my mind with ever new and increasing
wonder — the starry heavens above me, and the moral law
within me.
— Immanuel Kant

At the international level, Green politics have become a major
force for ecological change. Australia's United Tasmanian
Group, formed in 1972, and New Zealand's Values Party, formed
a few months later, were the first political parties with green
platforms to challenge established parliamentary systems. The
West German Greens (die Grunen) emerged in the early 1980s
from a mass movement that used direct action to confront local
community issues. They drew on people who had participated
in such "basis" movements as the anti-nuclear, ecology, women's
peace, urban squatters, gay rights, Third World solidarity, and
youth movements. They burst onto the international scene in
1983 when they won enough votes (5.6 per cent) to be seated
in the West German National Assembly (the *Bundestag*). In the
elections following the German reunification of 1990, the West
German Greens lost* their representation, but the East Germans
gained eight seats.

An emerging green movement is taking shape in the
commonwealth countries of the former Soviet Union and in
eastern Europe. In the Soviet Union, Stalin and Breznev had used
the slogan "Fight Nature." Industrialization targets that had to
be met every five years resulted in the rapid growth of heavy
industry with attendant environmental problems. But environmental activists, encouraged by former President Gorbachev's

---

*   *However, in the elections held in 1998, the Green Party has made a comeback and are*
now part of the ruling coalition in Germany — editors.

perestroika (restructuring) and glasnost (openness) programs, have pointed to structural problems in the Soviet economic planning process, as well as to pollution from industry, nuclear power, and public works construction.

In Hungary, growing citizen concern about environmental mismanagement broke out in 1988 over the planned construction of a series of dams on the Danube River. It was followed by local protests over air pollution in Budapest, the disposal of nuclear power plant wastes, and the effects of bauxite mining.

Polish citizens environmental movements have followed in the wake of Solidarity's labor movement. Farmers in the beautiful mountainous region around Rabka protested the planned expropriation of their traditional land holdings for redevelopment, arguing that the region's ecology and climate would be destroyed. Their protest was joined by members of the Polish Ecological Club and the Association of Polish City Planners and succeeded in halting the development.

A Yugoslavian Green Union was founded in 1988. It argued for alternative ecologically sound development, rather than the bandaids traditionally applied as environmental problems emerged. One hundred people demonstrated in Slovenia over the mismanagement of the environment and natural resources. By 1989 some 25 societies concerned with the environment had formed. Local issues have galvanized support among young people who are disenchanted with state-level environmental politics.

Green movements gained recognition in the Baltic republics of Lithuania, Latvia, and Estonia in 1988. The Lithuanian Green Movement comprises scientists, environmentalist and nationalists. In October 1988, 30,000 Lithuanians formed a 'ring of life' around a Chernobyl style nuclear reactor and then successfully petitioned for a shutdown. They have protested against pollution and promoted healthier food. Environmentalism is seen as a way to restore Lithuanian heritage and to press for independence from Moscow. The Green "Panda" ecology program in Estonia protests air pollution (in Sillamae workers must wear gas masks) and water pollution (in Tapa one can set fire to drinking water). It promotes natural limits, green education and green conscience.

Earth First!

Inspired by Ed Abbey, and founded by disenchanted environmentalist Dave Foreman in the early 1980s, Earth First! advocates strategic ecotage. Its Bible is Ecodefence: A Field Guide to Monkeywrenching and its medium of communication is Earth First! : The Radical Environmental Journal, which proclaims "no compromise in defense of Mother Earth."

Earth First!ers are not a organized movement in a formal sense. Rather they are a loose association of "earth warriors" dedicated to saving the wilderness through sabotaging the machines that destroy it. They are furious at the failure of the Forest Service and the Bureau of Land Management (BLM) to set aside America's last heritage of wilderness and at bureaucratic environmentalism for lack of aggressive action. Its methods are demonstrations, guerilla theater, civil disobedience, and monkey wrenching (ecological sabotage). Many in the movement consider themselves anarchists and all deny that they have been responsible for any injuries to human beings.

Earth First! direct actions include blockades of logging roads, tree-sits in old-growth forests, demonstrations outside of US Forest Service offices, lumber company sit-ins, and protests over the Smithsonian Institute's proposal to place an observatory in Arizona threatening the habitat of the Mount Graham red squirrel. In more notable nonviolent actions Earth First!ers have padlocked themselves to bulldozers, locked themselves to the cranes of log export ships to support US millworkers, entered their own grazing protest floats in ranchers' livestock parades, and scaled coliseum walls with protest banners.

But Earth First! has a philosophy that goes beyond simple direct actions in defense of the wilderness. For Foreman, it is essential that people maintain their evolutionary ties to the wild. "I am a product of the Pleistocene epoch, the age of large mammals," he holds. "I do not want to live in a world without jaguars and great blue whales and redwoods and rain forests, because this is my geological era, this is my family, this is my context. I only have meaning in situ, in the age I live in, the late Pleistocene."

According to Howie Wolke in 1982:

"Earth First! has its roots deeply embedded in the wilderness of the western U.S. We've recognized that wilderness preservation is the most urgent necessity on Earth. Once wilderness is gone, in most places geologic time will be needed for nature to restore it. And once the living organisms that depend on wilderness become extinct, they're gone forever.

I don't mean to downplay the importance of other aspects of the environmental struggle. But eventually, the gears of this civilization will grind to a halt under the immense weight of its own blundering and greed. And when this glorious day occurs, the sky will gradually return to blue, our imprisoned and polluted waters will once again begin to run free, and the suburbs will turn to dust as our population is forced – one way or another – to return to a manageable level. But it will all be for naught, unless we've had the vision and determination to save the wilderness and the wild things dependent upon it.

So, speak out with passion against the mindless insanity of nuclear proliferation; against killer acid rain; against toxic chemical wastes; against air you can see, water you can't drink; and above all, against the Earth-raping power-brokers of the multinationals and their governmental cohorts. But let Earth First! always concentrate its efforts on the wilderness battleground. It's where we can do the most good."

Green Peace

Using direct action and confrontation as strategies for change, Greenpeace, now the largest international environmental organization, takes on a variety of issues, from promoting nuclear--free seas, to saving whales and seals, to protesting the waste trade and toxics, and saving Antarctica. Beginning in 1971, it used the Quaker tradition of bearing personal witness to atrocities, such as sailing into Pacific nuclear test areas, and expanding the strategy to global witnessing through the mass media.

Greenpeace started its "save the whales" campaign in 1973 when a New Zealand biologist working in Vancouver liberated a killer whale from an aquarium. In 1975 volunteers in a rubber boat confronted Soviet whaling harpooners, capturing the event on film. After that moment of international recognition, it confronted whaling countries through the International Whaling Commission and organized boycotts and grassroots rallies. After ten years of protest only three countries Japan, Iceland, and Norway continue to harvest whales. Action against these holdouts continues and against the Whaling Commission's relaxation of whaling bans and quotas.

In the Pacific, after taking on the issue of nuclear-free seas, international attention was gained when the French sunk a protesting Greenpeace vessel, the Rainbow Warrior, in 1985, in New Zealand. Greenpeace continued to block and tag naval vessels carrying nuclear weapons and reported them through newspapers such as the New York Times. As a result, dozens of ports and nations banned ships carrying such weapons. Greenpeace activists also exposed

Box 14.1. **THE GREEN REAPERS VS. MONSANTO**

UK—On July 4, five women dressed in protective suits "openly and accountably" pulled up 200 genetically engineered sugar beets from a Monsanto "test field" at Model Farm, Oxfordshire.

Before they were arrested, the five members of the so-called GenetiX Snowball Campaign—Melanie Jarman, Rowan Tilly, Kathryn Tulip, Zoe Elford and Jo Hamilton—took care to seal the plants in clearly labeled bags "for disposal by the relevant authorities".

Two weeks later, the giant biotech company brought charges against the women, seeking to recover costs for "unlimited damages".

"This is a David and Goliath situation", declared Jarman. "Monsanto's bullying tactics are being used to distract attention from their flawed science."

The idea behind the GenetiX Snowball is that each protester is to encourage two new activists to visit one of Monsanto's 70 UK test fields and "pull up a maximum of 100 plants". Snowball actions are scheduled for the first and third weekends of every month.

On July 18, a band of seven women and men took the Snowball campaign to a test-field in Banbury where, to the delight of the activists, the farmer informed them that his crops were perfectly natural. He said that Monsanto officials had not told him that the canola seed he had contracted to grow was genetically engineered. When he found out, he withdrew from the program.

The women have claimed that the July 4 action is protected by a 1967 Criminal Law Act that allows "reasonable force" to be used to prevent a "crime"—the crime in this case being the pollution of wild plant communities with a "spill" of laboratory-engineered mutant organisms. In 1997, more than 12 million hectares were planted with gene-spliced seeds – a ten-fold increase from 1996. Norway has banned the import of suspect US soybeans and Austria and Luxembourg have enacted bans against Genetically Engineered (GE) foods. In Britain, Prince Charles has proclaimed that he will never purchase or consume any GE foods.

"A bunch of people are trying to get rich by telling us that nature isn't good enough and that we will have to take genes out of a fish and put them in a strawberry," a Swiss farmer named Kaspar Gunthardt told the *New York Times*. "They are changing the basic rules of life and they want to try it all out on us."

"The shadow of the Holocaust is dense and incredibly powerful still," University of Pennsylvania ethicist Arthur Caplan told the *Times*. "To [Europeans], the potential to abuse genetics is not theory. It is a historical fact."

" There has been no consultation with the British people as to their desire for GE food or crops," notes the Genetic Engineering network [PO Box 9656, London N44JY, www.dmac.co.uk/gen.] After a nationwide poll found that 77 percent of the GE produce is public opposed, Monsanto spent millions on a massive UK ad campaign to promote bio-engineered plants and food.

GenetiX Snowball has called for a five-year moratorium on the release of GE crops into the environment. According to Snowballer Peter Pritchard, "The use of the British people as guinea pigs and their countryside as a laboratory for the release of genetically modified organisms is an act of sheer recklessness."

Source : Genetix Snow ball campaign, Genetic Engg Network, P.O Box 9656, London, N44JY

ships carrying toxic wastes destined for dumps in Third World countries such as Guyana, Guinea, Honduras, the Bahamas, Panama and Tonga. Seventy-eight countries subsequently banned waste imports. In Antarctica, Greenpeace monitored trash, diesel fuel, and human waste that research stations dumped into the ocean and promoted the idea of a world park instead.

Like Earth First!, Greenpeace has attacked forms of industrial production that threaten the reproduction of life. Its efforts have thus focused on resolving the contradiction between production and reproduction. Its ethic is fundamentally biocentric – individual life forms, especially those valued by humans and saved through human witnessing, are sacred.

....

Earth Values

"And yet beings are rooted in me.
Behold the scheme of My sovereigrity!
Myself the origin and the support of
beings, yet standing apart from them..."

— *The Vedanta*

MOTHER EARTH

Over 100 years ago, the great Indian Chief, Seattle, was faced with the loss of his tribe's land. He responded out of his love and respect for the land, with utter honesty, and heartbreaking eloquence:

"We are part of the earth and it is part of us.
The perfumed flowers are our sisters;
The deer, the horse, the great eagle,
These are our brothers.
The rocky crests, the juices of the meadows,
The body heat of the pony, and man—
all belong to the same family.

So, when the Great Chief in Washington sends word
that he wishes to buy our land, he asks much of us

If we decide to accept, I will make one condition:
The white man must treat the beasts of this land
as his brothers.
I am a savage and do not understand any other way.
I have seen a thousand rotting buffalos on the prairie,
Left by the white man who shot them from a passing train.
I am a savage and I do not understand how the smoking
Iron horse can be more important than the buffalo
That we kill only to stay alive.

178

Where is man without the beasts?
If the beasts were gone, men would die
from a great loneliness of spirit.
For whatever happens to the beasts
Soon happens to man.
All things are connected,
This we know.
The earth does not belong to man;
man belongs to the earth.
This we know.
All things are connected
like the blood which unites one family.
All things are connected.
Whatever befalls the earth befalls the sons of the earth.
Man did not weave the web of life,
he is merely a strand in it.
Whatever he does to the web,
he does to himself."

Indigenous Peoples Recruit for the New Frontier

Christina Salat

The Indian ...stands free and unconstrained in Nature; her inhabitant and not her guest. But the civilized man has the habits of the house. His house is a prison.
— Henry David Thoreau

The ship called Earth on which we stand is sinking. The time to make better choices and insist on life rafts for all was yesterday. Can we put to rest the harmful priorities and prejudices of today and join land-based people in the fight for Earth's survival?

At the United Nations Earth Summit in 1992, world leaders met to discuss the environmental crisis but only one indigenous leader—Marcos Terena of the Terena Tribe in Brazil—was allowed to speak. He was allotted five minutes to represent the viewpoints of five thousand indigenous nations, all of which have never had a problem living sustainably with the planet.

Said Terena, "You cannot just squander millions and millions of dollars (on environmental conferences) if you don't want to listen to what the Earth has to tell you." Continued denial will prove fatal. Humanity's headlong pursuit of development at any cost has come at a price: we have built lives (for some) that are faster and fancier than any that have come before, at the cost of a planet that is growing less and less capable of sustaining any life at all. Ariel Araujo of the Mocovi Tribe in Argentina noted, "Indigenous peoples have the power to maintain the equilibrium that the planet needs to continue advancing. That is our technology, which is more advanced than the technology that money gives birth to."

Spurred into action by the lack of indigenous representation at the United Nations summit, Terena simultaneously organized the first ever World Gathering of Indigenous and Tribal Leaders. The Brazilian government donated land located within the compound of a psychiatric hospital, complete with patients. Ignoring the ironic (some might say racist) fact that, until 1978, indigenous people had the same human rights as the criminally insane, seven Amazon tribes built a village within the asylum to host the historical gathering.

Earth pioneers from the Americas, Asia, Africa, Australia, Europe and the Pacific Rim passed through the guarded checkpoints to reach the inaugural gathering, where the 109-point Kari-Oca Earth Charter was unanimously drafted and signed. This charter provides environmentally sound guidelines for human rights, biodiversity, conservation, development strategies, land and territory, culture, science and intellectual property. Said Helen Corbett of the Yamitji Tribe in Australia, "We come to reaffirm the practices that we have adopted since time immemorial to preserve Mother Nature.....We want to share that knowledge and understanding, educating the non-indigenous people throughout the world."

The indigenous Earth charter was made available to the United Nations and is available to anyone via the Internet at www.yakoana.com. So why, in this age of information superhighways, is it unfamiliar? Terena offers this explanation:

"This life code that no scientist has ever managed to unveil rests with the Indians. You don't have to look any further or research any further or spend millions of dollars on new research. We, the Indians would like to offer you our time, our wisdom, for your civilization. And once again, we have to ask you, are you prepared for that? Is the contemporary world prepared to listen to what we want to convey after five hundred years of silence?"

Loaded questions. How can we listen to one another when some of us are deafened by disdain, while others are filled with mistrust—and for historically good reason?

Where is the common ground between tribal people and the descendants of those who came bearing small pox-infected blankets and—according to accounts such as Toxic Waste and Racism in the U.S. and "Dances with Garbage" in the April 4, 1991, Newsweek—come again today bearing toxic waste? Where is the common ground between descendants of people enslaved and slave owners, between men and women with centuries of hate crimes between us, between humans and every other creature we brutally disregard? Is there common ground?

Yes. We are standing on it.

All life depends upon a healthy ecosystem. If planet Earth goes down, those of us with fast, fancy industrialized lives are no safer from extinction than those of us who have remained connected to the land. It will take all of us working together to turn around this ship. Are we willing? The fact that, worldwide, so many of us still fight for basic human rights as others of us continue to oppose equality says something about the oppressive nature that runs through our blood as a species. This critical human flaw is exactly what has allowed us to rush toward mass destruction because we do not—have not ever—valued all life enough to respect it. The time is now for a massive shift toward human kindness at any cost.

We of the industrial nations are dying from countless diseases of body and spirit, are more familiar with the insides of cars and buildings than the feel of the Earth and its elements, are more comfortable being intimate with the E-mail than with a flesh-and-blood neighbor. Instead of a life well lived, Prozac and other substances provide our link to inner peace. This is our final wake-up call. We cannot continue to make such choices if we are to

Box 15.1. **THE PENAN OF SARAWAK**

For thousands of years the Penan have lived in harmony with the forest, harvesting and not destroying the forest which sustains their survival. This is a society where women and men participate equally, maintaining the communal life in the forest.

In March 1987, thousands of indigenous people in Sarawak, Malaysia, formed human barricades across logging roads in the deep interior of the tropical rainforest. For more than 20 years, their forest has been ripped apart for logs which are predominantly exported to Japan.

Entire villages walked for days across the mountains to the logging roads which traverse their lands. While the men set up wooden fences and built rest shelters, the women wove leaves for roof thatch and organized food supplies. Breastfeeding mothers, old women, young children and men stood in vigil, stopping logging operations for almost seven months. The police and army forcibly dismantled the blockades and arrested some of the men. Blockades were set up again at the end of 1988, and in early January 1989 more than 100 Penan men were arrested under a newly created offence designed to criminalise the Penan's battle for their legitimate land rights. The women take over the responsibilities of the villages, seeking food and water supplies. Many have to stand by helplessly while their children have less and less to eat and polluted water causes diseases to increase.

The struggle of the Penan to maintain their culture and way of life is dismissed as 'primitive'. They are urged to join the mainstream and be 'developed'. But the reality is that no alternative is offered for the deprivation of their forest resources. Where resettlement has taken place in other native communities, the effects have been negative, leading to a breakdown in the community itself and a dependency on the cash economy.

Meanwhile arrest and intimidations continue, but the Penan refuse to give up. As the forest dwindles, the Penan have to walk for days to seek food and clean water. The land is their life. 'If we don't do something to protect the little that is left, there will be nothing for our children. Until we die we will block this road."

Source : Edited from Chee Yoke Ling, Friends of the Earth, Malaysia, Women, Environment, Development Seminar, Women's Environmental Network, March 1989.

survive. Indigenous leaders from the world's first gathering of land-based peoples agree. Said the Dalai Lama of Tibet, "Due to modern technology, sometimes a human being feels he is owner of this planet......This is a wrong conception." Ben Jugatan of the Ayta Tribe in the Philippines summarized simply: "Land is life."

Said Viktor Kaisepo of the Biak Tribe in West Papua, "What happened five hundred years ago in the Americas (the mass slaughtering of indigenous tribes by European colonists in order to claim and overdevelop Earth's resources), what happened two years ago in Australia, is happening in my country....If we want to protect our environment, our culture, then we will be considered by our government to be subversive."

Enter Ahn Crutcher, one United States subversive of European descent. With little media experience, no budget, and no time to raise one, Crutcher was told in 1992 that a serious effort to document the impending world gathering was impossible. Yet, she made her way to the newly erected village of Kari-Oca with cameras and crew. "Being disconnected from the soul of nature allows us to do soulless things," Crutcher said, "I think it's the root of all our other problems. I just wanted to help."

Crutcher intended to film the gathering only as a record for its participants. One-third of the people interviewed did not speak Spanish, Portuguese, or English so her crew recorded information they could not comprehend. After translation, they discovered the indigenous speakers were, in fact, translating the lost language of nature for all of us who have forgotten it.

And so Yakoana was born—a piece of history documented rather than ignored. The film provides a commentary on the future of our world from those who have always aimed to protect not its borders but its health. Yakoana's title refers to dust from the resin of a tree used by Yanomami shamans to perceive the breath of the planet. Woven together by Academy Award-winning editor Vivien Hillgrove (Henry and June, Blue Velvet, Amadeus, The Unbearable Lightness of Being), Yakoana gives voice to those who live with the Earth and calls upon us to join them. Said Crutcher:

"Indigenous people are using Yakoana in their fight to save nature. The documentary is getting individual classrooms of kids to think about whether cars and cities are bad. In my opinion, it doesn't have to be a win or lose situation, but our definition of winning does need to change. I would like to see the indigenous peoples' point of view on television, in schools and libraries, distributed worldwide via Greenpeace and Amnesty International...but right now it's just me with a lot of tapes on my kitchen table."

A few weeks after the gathering, the village of Kari-Oca was burned to the ground, most likely a result of political racism. Terena noted, however, that traditionally, when tribes moved on to allow the land to rest, villages were often burned to signify new beginnings, taking the next step.

Five years after the United Nations Earth Summit, there was Rio+5—the world's official environmental update. The prognosis: globally, things haven't improved much. Indigenous leaders have also conducted another gathering on December 1998. But environmental brainstorming—whether such gatherings are separate or united—is still just a first step. Said Vincent Johnson of the United States, Onondaga Nation, "In order for the people to help, it has to start with the individual. The individual's lifestyle would have to change in order to help out the environment."

Governments and corporations have always followed the lead of economic currency. If people insist on clean water, air and dirt, on healthy food, harmless fuel and human kindness, new empires will rise as others crumble. In order to demand such a global shift in priorities, however, it must first take place inside ourselves. We must make time in our busy lives to evolve.

The bleakest times are times when heroes step forward. Change starts, continues and succeeds with regular, stressed-out, pissed-off individuals like you and me. What can we do? Join together with those who support good in the world; apply peer pressure against shortsightedness, oppression, evil. Make every day Earth Day. Spend energy, money and time correcting the mess humankind has made.

But first, go outside and smell the Earth. Touch it. Taste it. Feel its breath. You can't fight for something you don't love. Is the common ground on which we live worth saving? If so, step forward. The frontiers of human decency are waiting to be explored.

....

The maidenflower
bends to every autumn wind
and I must wonder:
to whom does she give her heart
here in the late fall meadow?

— *Fujiwara No Tokihira.*

The Concept of Natural Value: A Theory for Environmental Ethics

Holmes Rolston III

For we cannot command Nature, except by obeying her
— Francis Bacon

After a long study of the possibility of the evolution of biological molecules capable of self organization, Manfred Eigen, a thermo-dynamics expert, concludes "that the evolution of life. . . must be considered an inevitable process despite its indeterminate course." But we hardly know whether to put it that strongly, since nothing suggests much coding for life in the microscopic particles as such, and life is presumably quite rare in the universe. Still, life does seem to be some sort of accident waiting to happen. Astronomers speak with excitement of the "anthropic principle", which holds that the universe is constructed with a tendency to evolve life and mind. At the same time, evolutionary biologists can be adamant that nothing in evolutionary theory guarantees the ascent of ever more complex forms.

For environmental ethics, "anthropic principle" is an unfor-tunately chosen term, one that no ecologist would have selected. We wish to avoid associating anthropocentrism with the process, especially any suggestion that everything in the universe is arranged to produce and serve humans. But what the anthropic principle points to is important—a rich, fertile nature that is energetic and creative, so much so that at length nature evolves life and mind. That may involve some accident, but it cannot be all accident; it is in some sense a property, a potential of systemic nature that it projects natural history.

David Hume claimed that nature has no more regard to good above ill than to heat above cold, or to drought above moisture, or to light above heavy. Or to life above non-life, he probably would have added. That indifference can seem true in the short range, though day-to-day nature is an impressive life-support system. Sometimes it even seems true in the long range: every organism dies; species go extinct. Nature doesn't care.

Yet nature has spun quite a story, first in the heavens and later on Earth, making this planet with its landscapes, seascapes and going from zero to five million species in five billion years. Perhaps to say that nature "has regard" for life is the wrong way of phrasing it; we do not want to ascribe purpose to nature. At the same time, something is going on—systematically, historically. We live in what K. G. Denbigh calls "an inventive universe." We comfort a projective nature, one restlessly full of projects––stars, comets, planets, moons and also rocks, crystals, rivers, canyons, seas. The life in which these astronomical and geological processes culminate is still more impressive, but it is of a piece with the whole projective system. Everything is made out of dirt and water, stellar stuff and funded with stellar energy. One cannot be impressed with life in isolation from its originating matrix. Nature is a fountain of life, and the whole fountain—not just the life that issues from it—is of value. Nature is genesis, Genesis.

Values in Projective, Systemic Nature

Environmental ethics asks: What is an appropriate attitude toward such a projective system? Has it any value? Any claim on human behavior? Ethics begins in interactions between persons and at this scope nature is a resource. At first it seems right to say that our duties are to persons, and that dirt, water, air, minerals, rivers, landscapes are instrumental in such duty. But there comes a point in environmental ethics when we ask about our *sources*, not just our *resources*. The natural environment is discovered to be the womb in which we are generated and which we really never leave. That is the original meaning of nature, from the Latin *natans*, giving birth, Mother Earth.

Nonbiotic things have no information in them, no genome, much less sentience or experience. There are no cells, no organs, no skin, no metabolisms. Impressed with the display of life and personality on Earth, we correctly attach most of our ethical concern to persons and to organisms; but we may incorrectly assume that mere things are beyond appropriate and inappropriate consideration.

A "mere thing" can, however, be something to be respected, the project of projective nature. Crystals, volcanoes, geysers, headlands, rivers, springs, moons, cirques, paternoster lakes, buttes, mesas, canyons—these also are among the natural kinds. They do not have organic integrity or individuality; they are constantly being built, altered, their identity in flux. But they are recognizably different from their background and surroundings. They may have striking particularity, symmetry, harmony, grace, story, spatiotemporal unity and continuity, even though they are also diffuse, partial, broken. They do not have wills or interests but rather headings, trajectories, traits, successions, beginnings, endings, cycles, which give them a tectonic integrity. They can be projects (products) of quality. The question now is not "Can they suffer?" or "Is it alive?" but "What deserves appreciation?"

In nature there is a negentropic constructiveness in dialectic with an entropic teardown, a model of working for which we hardly yet have an adequate scientific, much less a valuational, theory. Yet this is nature's most striking feature, one that ultimately must be valued and of value. In one sense, we say (with Hume) that nature is indifferent to planets, mountains, rivers and trilliums. But in a more profound sense nature has bent toward making and remaking these objects (=projects), and millions of other kinds, for several billion years. These performances are worth noticing—remarkable, memorable—and they are worth noticing not just because of their tendencies to produce something else, certainly not merely because of their tendency to produce this noticing in certain recent subjects, our human selves. They are loci of value so far as they are products of systemic nature in its formative processes. The opening movements of a symphony contribute to the power of the finale, but they are not merely of instrumental value; they are of value for what they are in themselves. The splendors of the heavens and the marvels of Earth do not lie simply in their roles as a fertilizer for life or a stimulator of experience. There is value wherever there is positive creativity.

In Mammoth Cave, in a section named Turner Avenue, there are rooms laden with gypsum crystals spun as fine threads, a rare formation known as "angel hair". So fragile are these needles that humans passing through and disturbing the air destroy the hair-thin filaments. This part of the cave is closed, never visited by tourists and only on exceptional occasions by mineralogists. A nonbiotic work of nature (a kind of dirt!) is here protected at the cost of depriving humans of access to it. This park policy is partly for humanistic reasons: to preserve angel hair for scientific research. But it also involves an appreciation of angel hair as a project of systemic nature. Angel hair counts morally in the sense that natural value here lays a claim on human behavior.

Mount Rushmore, South Dakota, has been carved into a monument to national pride with the faces of four presidents and has provoked a response at nearby Crazy Horse, a (partially completed) mountain-sized Indian on his horse. Stone Mountain, Georgia, is a monument to the Old South. Christo built of white fabric a twenty-five-mile-long, eighteen-foot-high, artistic *Running Fence* over California ranchland, range, cliffs and seashore, ending in the sea. The cost was $3 million and the fence was taken down after a few weeks.

Some claim that such environmental artworks provide positive aesthetic experience in stark polarity with virgin nature. Any damage to the environment, whether to ecosystems, wildlife or scenery, is justified by the positive drama of big-scale art in antithesis/synthesis with nature. These artists may not be claiming that virgin nature is aesthetically bad or neutral; to the contrary, they want the natural scene as a support and contrast for their works. Where these works are ephemeral, they can perhaps be tolerated. Their environmental impact is thereby reduced, although they may still be an aesthetic affront to nature. But where they mar landscapes, mountains, deserts, what they do is of moral concern because destruction of value is wrong. At least the burden of proof lies with the artists to show that their complex of art and nature augments values present.

We may not want any more summit roads up fourteeners, or fun-bridges over gorges, or carved-up mountains, firefalls, valley curtains, soap in geysers, or names written over rock cliffs or stalagmites, because a developing environmental ethics insists that there is a better way to behave at these places, one that recognizes their site integrity and accepts them as givens of projective nature. We will leave the pyramids on the sands of Egypt for historic reasons but oppose carving a president's face on Yosemite's Half Dome. These are questions of right conduct. We will say that humans can have no duties to clouds or dust devils, even though these are temporary aggregations with enough identity for us to say where they start and stop. They have little integrated process in them. But toward other projects in nature there is irresponsible (inappropriately responsive) behavior.

An Endangered Ethic?

When an ethicist compares a description of Earth's biological history with the threatened human disruption of Earth's adventure, human activities seem misfit in the system. Although humans are maximizing their own species interests, and in this respect behaving as does each of the other species, they do not have any adaptive fitness. They are not really fitting into the evolutionary processes of ongoing biological conservation and elaboration. They are not really dynamically stable in their ecosystems. Humans do not transcend their own interests to become moral overseers. They do not follow nature, evaluating what is going on. Yet contemporary ethical systems limp when they try to prescribe right conduct here. They too seem misfits in the roles most recently demanded of them.

The most common cause of extinction in spontaneous nature is for a species to fall into the ever deepening ruts of overspecialization. Homo Sapiens has proved remarkably unspecialized and seems in no danger of extinction. Still, there is something over-specialized about an ethic, held by the dominant class of Homo Sapiens that regards the welfare of only one of several million species as an object and beneficiary of duty.

There is nothing wrong with humans exploiting their environment, resourcefully using it. Nature requires this of every species, humans not excepted. What *is* the case—that humans must consume their environment—*ought to be so*: humans ought to consume their environment. But humans have options about the extent to which they do so; they also have, or ought to have, a conscience about it. The consumption of individual animals and plants is one thing; it can be routinely justified. But the consumption of species is something else; it cannot be routinely justified. To the contrary, each species made extinct is forever slain and each extinction incrementally erodes the regenerative powers on our planet.

If this requires a paradigm change about the sorts of things to which duty can attach, so much the worse for those humanistic ethics no longer functioning in, or suited to their changing environment. The anthropocentrism associated with them was fiction anyway. There is something Newtonian, not yet Einsteinian, as well as something morally naive, about living in a reference frame where one species takes itself as absolute and values everything else relative to its utility. Such limited theories can become true only when they learn their limits.

Concluding a survey of paleontology, D. V. Ager writes, "The history of any one part of the earth, like the life of a soldier, consists of long periods of boredom and short periods of terror." Boredom is not the most apt description of the long routines of evolutionary speciation but the mass extinctions were certainly periods of terror. Of late, in the most recent chapter in the story, humankind is the great terror—but a terror with a conscience. Turned in on itself to value the human species alone, this conscience makes humankind only a greater terror. Turned outward to accept duties to species and to the ecosystemic Earth, this conscience could make humans the noblest species and give them a more inclusive environmental fitness.

....

Nature with equal mind,
Sees all her sons at play;
Sees Man control the wind,
The wind sweep Man away.
— *Matthew Arnold*

Global Action Plan

"Could you can I with fate conspire
To grasp this sorry scheme of things entire,
would not we shatter it to bits—and then
Remould it nearer to the heart's desire!"

— *Omar Khayyam*

An Appeal for the Future generations

Hello, I'm Severn Suzuki, speaking for ECHO — the Environmental Children's Organization.

We are a group of four 12 and 13-year-olds from Canada trying to make a difference: Vanessa Suttie, Morgan Geisler, Michelle Quigg and me.

We raised all the money ourselves to come 6000 miles to tell you adults you must change your ways.

Coming up here today, I have no hidden agenda. I am fighting for my future. Losing my future is not like losing an election or a few points on the stock market.

I am here to speak for all generations yet to come. I am here to speak on behalf of the starving children around the world whose cries go unheard. I am here to speak for the countless animals dying across this planet — because they have nowhere left to go. We can't afford not to be heard.

I am afraid to go out in the sun now because of the holes in the ozone. I am afraid to breathe the air because I do not know what chemicals are in it. I used to go fishing in Vancouver with my dad, until just a few years ago we found the fish full of cancers. And now we hear about animals and plants going extinct every day — vanishing forever.

In my life, I have dreamed of seeing the great herds of wild animals, jungles and rainforests full of birds and butterflies, but now I wonder if they will even exist for my children to see.

Did you have to worry about these little things when you were my age?

All this is happening before our eyes and yet we act as if we have all the time we want and all the solutions.

I am only a child and I do not have all the solutions, but I want you to realize: neither do you! You do not know how to fix the holes in our ozone layer. You do not know how to bring salmon back up a dead stream. You do not know how to bring back an animal now extinct. And you cannot bring back the forests that once grew where there is now desert. If you do not know how to fix it, please stop breaking it!

Here, you may be delegates of your governments, business people, organizers, reporters or politicians — but really you are mothers and fathers, brothers and sisters, aunts and uncles — and all of you are somebody's child.

I am only a child, yet I know we are all part of a family, five billion strong, in fact, 30 million species strong, and we all share the same air, water and soil — borders and governments will never change that.

I am only a child, yet I know we are all in this together and should act as one single world towards one single goal. In my anger, I am not blind, and in my fear, I am not afraid to tell the world how I feel.

In my country, we make so much waste; we buy and throw away, buy and throw away, and yet Northern countries will not share with the needy. Even when we have more than enough, we are afraid to lose some of our wealth, afraid to share. In Canada, we live the privileged life, with plenty of food, water and shelter — we have watches, bicycles, computers and television sets.

Two days ago here in Brazil, we were shocked when we spent some time with some children living on the streets. And this is what one child told us: "I wish I was rich, and if I were, I would give all the street children food, clothes, medicine, shelter, and love and affection."

If a child on the street who has nothing, is willing to share, why are we who have everything still so greedy?

I cannot stop thinking that these children are my age; that it makes a tremendous difference where you are born; that I could be one of those children living in the *favelas* (slums) of Rio. I could be a child starving in Somalia, a victim of war in the Middle East or a beggar in India.

I am only a child, yet I know if all the money spent on war was spent on ending poverty and finding environmental answers, what a wonderful place this Earth would be!

At school, even in kindergarten, you teach us to behave in the world. You teach us not to fight with others, to work things out, to respect others, to clean up our mess, not to hurt other creatures, to share — not be greedy.

Then why do you go out and do the things you tell us not to do?

Do not forget why you are attending these conferences, who you are doing this for — we are your own children. You are deciding what kind of a world we will grow up in.

Parents should be able to comfort their children by saying, "everything's going to be all right, we are doing the best we can" and "it is not the end of the world." But I don't think you can say that to us anymore. Are we even on your list of priorities?

My dad always says, "You are what you do, not what you say." Well, what you do makes me cry at night.

You grown-ups say you love us. I challenge you: please make your actions reflect your words. Thank you for listening.

Severn Cullis-Suzuki, Earth Island Journal, Summer 1994.

Severn Cullis-Suzuki, then 12 years old, delivered this speech in 1992 at the Plenary Session of the UN Earth Summit in Rio de Janeiro, Brazil. She received a standing ovation.

••••

Common Principles for a Responsible and United World*

The philosophers have only interpreted the world in various ways. The point, however, is to change it.
— *Karl Marx*

We contend that we are not facing an inescapable situation and that the gravity of the threats or the complexity of the challenges before us should give rise to determination, not renunciation. Populations and human societies are endowed with the capacity to project their future and they possess quantities of principles to guide their choices and decisions.

The following few principles, which were formulated in such a way as to take into account the diversity of our cultures and societies, appear as essential references at the present time.

The conservation principle: The Earth we inherited from our ancestors is not for us alone; we also owe it to future generations. Neither our special place on the planet Earth nor our technical know-how entitle us to deplete its resources and destroy it unchecked. The expansion of science and technology has given us a new freedom. This freedom must go hand in hand with a sense of reverence with regard to nature, the limitations and cycles of which we must respect and the essential assets of which we must protect: water, air, soil, seas and oceans, living species and the major balances necessary to life. Accordingly, human societies would orient their progress toward production models and lifestyles that do not deplete or squander resources, nor dump waste that may harm the essential equilibria of local or global environments.

---

* (reproduced from the Alliance For a Responsible and United World, published by the Charles Leopold Mayer Foundation for the Progress of humankind (FPH), Switzerland)
— editors

The Humanity principle: The humanity of humankind can only truly be measured by: the possibility for each individual to possess the essentials of life and to live in dignity, respect, equity and solidarity among people and among societies; and its respect for nature and all living species.

The responsibility principle: Individuals, enterprises, states and international organizations alike must assume their responsibilities in the development of harmony within societies, among people and between human beings and their environment; they must do so in accordance with their resources and powers. People are jointly responsible for the fate of humankind.

The moderation principle: We must learn to curb our cupidity. The wealthiest, who are caught in the spiral of waste, must reform their lifestyles, moderate their consumption and learn frugality.

The caution principle: Human societies must wait to have acquired the ability to control present and future risks before they implement new products or new techniques.

The diversity principle: The diversity of cultures, as well as that of living beings, is a common asset, which is all people's duty to preserve; the diversity of civilizations is the best guarantee for humankind's capacity to invent responses geared to the infinite diversity of situations, challenges and environments; the planet's genetic resources must be protected, while respecting the communities that have protected and enhanced them hitherto.

The citizenship principle: We must learn to respect ourselves and to consider all human beings as full members of the vast human community.

In response to those who tend to see the world only in terms of the interplay between private interests, powers and market forces, it is good to reassert these few principles and to use them as guidelines to determine priorities and lay down strategies.

The Need for a Global Strategy

Many positive reactions have emerged to the three crises (infulfilled basic needs, squandered resources, untapped potentials of humans through work & creativity) humankind is facing. They range from specific exemplary actions in villages, towns and cities to the recent international conventions, from the charters or environmental audits drawn up or conducted by certain firms

---

Box 17.1. UNESCO GUIDELINES FOR ENVIRONMENTAL EDUCATION

Concern for deterioration in our environment caused by an indiscriminate use of various resources is not very recent altogether, even though its organized expression has gained momentum in the last decade. Recently, efforts have been initiated to impart environmental education through the channels of formal education in its early stages, particularly at primary and secondary levels.

Sustained efforts are yet to be made in integrating environmental education with non-formal education. The UNESCO drew up a set of guidelines for incorporating environmental education within the general framework of education.

The Tbilisi Declaration together with two of the recommendations of the Conference constitutes the framework, principles and guidelines for environmental education at all levels—local, national, regional and international—and for all age groups both inside and outside the formal school system.

Recommendations

I.   The Conference recommends the adoption of certain criteria which will help to guide efforts to develop environmental education at the national, regional and global levels: It felt that—

— Whereas it is a fact that biological and physical features constitute the natural basis of the human environment, its ethical, social, cultural and economic dimensions also play their part in determining the lines of approach and the instruments whereby people may understand and make better use of natural recources in satisfying their needs.

— Environmental education is the result of the reorientation and dovetailing of different disciplines and educational experiences which

to the energy policies decided upon in certain countries and forms of agriculture.

Such progress, however, still seems very limited and isolated compared to the major forces driving our world. Deep feelings of powerlessness prevail today. Each society, considered separately, appears to be paralyzed by the scale of the changes that need to be made. Each individual, enterprise and state senses

facilitate an integrated perception of the problems of the environment, enabling more rational action, capable of meeting social needs, to be taken.

— A basic aim of environmental education is to succeed in making individuals and communities understand the complex nature of the natural and the built environments resulting from the interaction of their biological, physical, social, economic and cultural aspects, and require the knowledge, values, attitudes and practical skills to participate in a responsible and effective way in anticipating and solving environmental problems, and in the management of the quality of the environment.

— A further basic aim of environmental education is clearly to show the economic, political and ecological interdependence of the modern world, in which decisions and actions by the different countries can have international repercussions. Environmental education should, in this regard, help to develop a sense of responsibility and solidarity among countries and regions as the foundation for a new international order which will guarantee the conservation and improvement of the environment.

— Special attention should be paid to understanding the complex relations between socio-economic development and the improvement of the environment.

— For this purpose, environmental education should provide the necessary knowledge for interpretation of the complex phenomena that shape the environment, encourage those ethical, economic and esthetic values which, constituting the basis of self-discipline, will further the development of conduct compatible with the preservation and improvement of the environment; it should also provide a wide range of practical skills required in the devising and application of effective solutions to environmental problems.

— To carry out these tasks, environmental education should bring about a closer link between educational processes and real life, building its activities around the environmental problems that are faced by particular communities and focusing analysis on these by means of an interdisciplinary, comprehensive approach which will permit a proper understanding of environmental problems.

— Environmental education should cater to all ages and socio-professional groups in the population. It should be addressed to (a) the general non-specialist public of young people and adults whose daily conduct has decisive influence on the preservation and improvement of the environment; (b) to particular social groups whose professional activities affect the quality of the environment; and (c) to scientists and technicians whose specialized research and work will lay the foundations of knowledge on which education, training and efficient management of the environment should be based.

— To achieve the effective development of environmental education, full advantage must be taken of all public and private facilities available to society for the education of the population the formal education system, different forms of non-formal education, and the mass media.

— To make an effective contribution towards improving the environment, educational action must be linked with legislation, policies, measures of control and the decisions that governments may adopt in relation to the human environment.

II.   The Conference endorses the following goals and objectives as guiding principles for environmental education:

Goals of Environmental Education

— to foster clear awareness of, and concern about, economic, social, political and ecological interdependence in urban and rural areas;

— to provide every person with opportunities to acquire the knowledge, values, attitudes, commitment and skills needed to protect and improve the environment;

— to create new patterns of behavior of individuals, groups and society as a whole towards the environment.

The categories of environmental education objectives are : *Awareness*: to help social groups and individuals acquire an awareness and sensitivity to the total environment and its allied problems.

Knowledge: to help social groups and individuals gain a variety of experience in, and acquire a basic understanding of, the environment and its associated problems.

Attitudes: to help social groups and individuals acquire a set of values and feelings of concern for the environment and the motivation for actively participating in environmental improvement and protection.

Skills: to help social groups and individuals acquire the skills for identifying and solving environmental problems.

Participation: to provide social groups and individuals with an opportunity to be actively involved at all levels in working toward the resolution of environmental problems.

Guiding principles: environmental education should:

— consider the environment in its totality—natural and built, techno-logical and social (economic, political, cultural-historical, moral, esthetic);

— be a continuous lifelong process, beginning at the preschool level and continuing through all formal and nonformal stages;

— be interdisciplinary in its approach, drawing on the specific content of each discipline in making possible a holistic and balanced perspective;

— examine major environmental issues from local, national, regional and international points of view so that students receive insights into environmental conditions in other geographical areas;

— focus on current and potential environmental situations while taking into account the historical perspective;

— promote the value and necessity of local, national and international cooperation in the prevention and solution of environmental problems; explicitly consider environmental aspects in plans for development and growth;

— enable learners to have a role in planning their learning experiences and provide an opportunity for making decisions and accepting their consequences;

— relate environmental sensitivity, knowledge, problem-solving skills and values clarification to every age, but with special emphasis on environmental sensitivity to the learner's own community in early years;

— help learners discover the symptoms and real causes of environ-mental problems;

— emphasize the complexity of environmental problems and thus the need to develop critical thinking and problem-solving skills;

— utilize diverse learning environments and a broad array of educa-tional approaches to teaching/learning about and from the environment with due stress on practical activities and first-hand experience.

Source : Final report of Inter-governmental Conference on Environmental Education, organized by UNESCO, in cooperation with UNEP, Tbilisia, Georgia, 14 – 26 October 1997.

the need to act, but is resigned to doing nothing and waiting for others to initiate actions, or decisions to be made elsewhere. Science, technology and the market have become the new names of fate, while ideologies and institutions, because they are slow to change, are often ill-equipped to deal with the present emergencies and challenges.

We must not be timid. Our duty is to be bold. We must chart a desireable future from all the different future scenarios possible on the basis of our common values; we must then design a consistent set of actions that will meet today's emergencies and can meet tomorrow's challenges. Just as the three crises are inseparable, so are the responses to them.

We do not believe that a sustainable development respecting the major ecological balances can be achieved at the price of the exclusion of a large part of humankind. We are wary of attempts to solve the problems we are facing through a relentless progression of technology and through restrictions imposed by the powerful few, and endured by the masses. We are convinced that the actions that need to be taken must aim at building balanced relations between people and their environments, in their full complexity and diversity, and at building balanced relations between people and their societies. The problem is not to establish a scale of gravity among the three crises, but to find forms of action that help to resolve them simultaneously. This convergence, along with the enactment of the seven principles listed above, must be our main guide in establishing action strategies. The world we want to build is truly a responsible and united world.

To meet this objective, we have no choice but to mobilize exceptional resources and determination. This is possible. The Western world emerged from the Big Depression of the 1930's thanks to an unprecedented mobilization of resources to prepare, and then wage World War II. At the close of this century, our proposal is to engage equivalent resources to combat all forms of poverty and exclusion, and to implement technologies and production models that respect our living environments.

As things stand today, 20% of the people own more than 80% of the world's wealth. Some families have an income equivalent to the resources of hundreds of thousands, perhaps millions, of deprived families. The vastly wealthy people and countries of the world will therefore have to bear the bulk of the effort.

Once this solidarity drive is clearly accepted, it will constitute the political condition on which all countries will be able to draw up common objectives and a consistent strategy. It will be the tangible expression of the recognition of the human community's unity. It may also be a key stage in the introduction of new mechanisms of solidarity and redistribution, similar to those that human societies have occasionally invented in the past.

Finally, for this strategy to succeed, it must be as consistent and complete as the present development model; it will require organizations, leaders, regulations and technologies geared to the given objectives. It will develop over time, at the price of unswerving determination.

From 1986 to 1993, the Charles Leopold Mayer Foundation for the Progress of Humankind (FPH), an independent Swiss foundation, backed a small group that had formed to reflect upon the challenges raised by the coming century and how these could be met. In 1988, the group, which called itself the Vezelay Group, launched a Call for a World States-General. As the group began to open up and international contacts were established, the Alliance was born. The FPH is backing its development.

....

Earthkeeping: The Politics of a Sustainable Future

Lamont C. Hempel

A nation without the means of reform is without means of survival
— *Edmund Burke*

If there is a meaningful way to harness both global and community sensibilities on behalf of environmental concerns, it will most likely involve a blending of the visions of catastrophists and optimizers. The combination of the catastrophist's alarms and the optimizer's bounded rationality may offer the best hope for effective action. Glocal* perspectives are more likely to emerge if a proper sense of urgency about world problems is cultivated and accompanied by a pragmatic sense of personal responsibility to act. Personal responsibility and action, however, is best cultivated within families and local communities. Hence the argument for re-establishing roots in community. A strengthened capacity for civic engagement may be absolutely essential for the development of a glocal system of environmental governance.

Beyond civic engagement lies the challenge of establishing a form of "civic environmentalism" (John Deluitt, 1994) that can supplement and complement other forms of engagement in the social, religious, cultural and political life of communities. Civic environmentalism represents a bottom up approach to problem solving that requires decentralized action and innovation within a centralized system of collaboration and coordination. In such

---

* *The word 'glocal' is derived from 'global' and 'local'. Although used by the author since the late 1980's, it appears to have originated and publicized in Japan — editors.*

a system, communities and other subnational political units would be encouraged to design and implement their own environmental programs, relying primarily on nonregulatory tools of education, grants, monitoring, technical assistance and public service programs that foster decentralized collaboration. To be sure, national, regional or global authority and standards must be allowed to override local programs in cases where they conflict with transboundary environmental protection. The burden of proof to justify intervention, however, would be placed on the shoulders of more centralized authorities. Ideally, the principle of subsidiarity would remain operative to keep deliberative processes working at the lowest appropriate level of governance.

Implicit in the foregoing discussion is the strong bias of glocal thinking toward a federal structure of governance. Limited experiments with world federalism may offer the best chance for balancing humanity's dual needs for unity and diversity. In such experiments lies the promise of a democratic means for equalizing the power of roots and wings in our lives. Federal designs that are confined to environment and security issues appear to be the most promising experiments for consideration, but even such limited challenges to the sovereign state system are likely to meet with overwhelming opposition. Geopolitics will continue to place enormous obstacles in the way to proposals for glocal governance.

The political limbo in which the United Nations is often forced to operate is suggestive of just how deeply the antipathy toward supranational arrangements is felt. Given the United Nations' many failed peacekeeping missions, such as in Somalia and Bosnia in 1994, is there any reason to be optimistic about the United Nations' global capability to conduct successful earthkeeping missions? Developing support for a stronger international confederation, let alone federation, is very difficult at this point in history. But must we assume that "what is past is prologue?" As evidence accumulates that continuation of today's geopolitics may irreparably damage the planet's life-support system, how can it truly be in any state's interest to defend the status quo?

Whether one adopts a cornucopian, catastrophist or optimizer perspective, the political future of planet earth is likely to be decided by forces that are global in nature but experienced as local problems and opportunities. For many people, concerns about the state of the planet's health are unlikely to seem any more pressing than those related to the economy, crime, ethnic conflict or many other issues. And for the nearly two billion human beings living at or near subsistence levels, basic needs for food, clothing and housing may drown out environmental concerns altogether. Policy agendas seem packed with urgent issues requiring action. The shifting attention given to environmental problems by the media and by governments may only reinforce a growing public perception that world events have outrun our political capacity to plan and manage. Rational ignorance may be a predictable result of having so many concerns to deal with. It fosters an understandable tendency for many to retreat from the turbulent world of politics and policy and to "freeride", as economists would say, on the hard work of those who remain engaged in solving the vexing problems of global interdependence.

Most people seem weary from the repeated failures of their institutions to keep pace with the changes wrought by technology, politics and population growth. Many appear deeply cynical about the possibilities of governing under such conditions, particularly when their trust in political leadership is very low and their opportunities for withdrawing from civic responsibilities, at least in the North, are multiplying with the speed of cable television channels. Perhaps catastrophism is an outlook that reflects the popular understanding of politics and government more than it does the perception of trends in global ecology.

The deadly combination of cynicism and consumerism pervading many human societies today threatens to leave us with a world devoid of such things as ancient forests, pure water, clean air and inspiring landscapes. While it is clear that many people will not rue the loss of such natural amenities, a disturbing question remains: Can humanity afford—economically, psychologically and politically—to reconstruct the world in ways that systematically destroy the natural heritage on which so much of human aesthetics, identity formation and general satisfaction depend? Can we in fact be human, in the fullest meaning of the term, without a rich and diverse natural environment in which to exist?

Unfortunately for hard-pressed defenders of rainforests, wildlife and other forms of natural capital, saving the environment may not be possible without first saving the polis. Investments in social capital and the community roots that feed it are key prerequisites in this regard. Global environmental governance is unlikely to succeed without prior and deeper commitments to local forms of deliberative democracy. On the other hand, environmental dilemmas may provide the key stimuli for fostering deliberation about the ways we govern ourselves. The public spirit nurtured by participation in democratic deliberation may be the only viable force behind hope for a sustainable future. That spirit must reflect concerns about both natural and social forms of capital. Their thoughtful integration is vital to the mission of earthkeeping.

....

Proposal for the United Nations to Declare the Twenty First Century as The Century of Restoring the Earth

Alan W. Teathestone

It's time for a change
— John Dewey, Campaign slogan

Sustainable development is now recognised as an important goal by politicians, conservationists, aid workers, planners and many other people. However, for sustainable development to be achieved, the world requires, first of all, to have sustainable ecosystems, as all our human well-being and wealth ultimately derives from the ability of our planet to provide abundance — clean air, fresh water, healthy food and natural resources which can be used to make products for people's benefit.

At present, we do not have sustainable ecosystems in the world—everywhere forests, wetlands, savannas etc. are being depleted, fragmented and destroyed. This is resulting in problems such as desertification, famine and starvation, soil erosion and extinction of species. It is also a contributory factor in global warming. Even if all the destruction currently taking place in the world were miraculously to stop tomorrow, we would still be left with a planet whose ability to support life—both human and that of the estimated 5 million other species in the world—is seriously diminished.

To return our planet to a state of health again, the current efforts to prevent further destruction (which in themselves are vital) must be matched by a concerted program of restoration, to help the Earth heal, and to ensure that there is a sustainable future for ourselves, and all our fellow species.

Most environmental initiatives are by necessity concentrated on 'damage limitation' – reducing the destructive impact our industrial culture has on the world, but because of this they tend to be adversarial, creating opposition and polarity amongst different people and interest groups. By contrast, restoration is an entirely positive activity which can, and often does, draw together people from different backgrounds behind the common task of doing something positive for their local area and therefore the planet. In recent years, numerous restoration programs have been initiated by local people, covering such diverse initiatives and ecosystems as the dry tropical forests of Costa Rica, the Caledonian forest in Scotland, the mangroves of Vietnam, salmon populations in rivers in the Pacific Northwest of the USA and the reintroduction of beavers to 13 countries in Europe.

However, in the 21st century, restoration on a substantially larger scale will become a major necessity on every continent and in every country. Because environmental degradation is a global phenomenon, which transcends cultural, political and national differences, restoration will provide an opportunity to unite all of humanity behind a shared goal—the first in our history—of helping to heal the Earth.

To catalyse this process, we are proposing to the United Nations that the 21st Century be declared the Century of Restoring the Earth, in the same way that, for example, 1986 was declared the International Year of Peace, and that the 1990s have been declared the Third Disarmament Decade.

Given the scale of the world's environmental problems today, restoration of degraded ecosystems will take at least a hundred years (and much longer in some cases—for example, restoring native forests to a primary condition), so it is entirely appropriate that a century-long perspective be taken for this.

The beginning of the new millennium is being looked upon by many as a significant time in the world's history. Possibly, the most important initiative which would mark it as a true turning point for humanity is to dedicate the 21st century to repairing the damage which has been wrought upon the planet, particularly in the last 150 years. Starting the new millennium with an international focus on restoration will provide a positive vision for nations and individuals to rally behind and will help people everywhere to realise that we need to actively take care of our degraded world for our future wellbeing.

Some possible initiatives to begin the Century of Restoring the Earth

10% of each nation's military budget to be re-directed to restoration activities. This percentage to be increased continuously in the years ahead. Military personnel, equipment and organisational abilities to be made available for key restoration programs. This will help to provide a new, meaningful role for the military in the next century, as true global security depends on having a healthy planet to live on! (Examples of this already exist—the RAF base at Kinloss, Moray, Scotland, has helped with the reintroduction of the sea eagle to Scotland by transporting young birds from Norway in their planes).

Establishment of an Earth Restoration Service, enrolling young people from all over the world as volunteers in essential restoration programs. This would be an expanded, international equivalent of the US Peace Corps or Britain's VSO (Voluntary Service Overseas), but focussed specifically on restoration. It would achieve practical restoration results and also provide training to local people wherever it operated in basic restoration principles and techniques. A similar scheme to this—the Earth Restoration Corps—has already been proposed as part of the

Agenda 21 initiative arising from the 1992 Earth Summit in Rio de Janeiro, Brazil.

Establishment of a Global Restoration Network, linking up existing restoration programs and initiatives so that they can exchange information, experience, techniques and skills. This would also provide a source of information and inspiration for new restoration projects and for people who want to become involved in restoration programs.

Establishment of few key 'flagship' projects, which would be visionary in scale and purpose, and which would capture the public imagination, rallying them around the whole concept of the 21st century being dedicated to the healing of the Earth. Possibilities for this include: a large scale, coordinated program of native forest restoration in the Sahel region of Africa, using native tree species to reverse the spread of desertification and the recurrent famines there; a concerted campaign to remove all land mines around the world by a specified target date; habitat restoration programs for 'charismatic' wildlife species, such as the tiger, panda etc., to ensure that these species survive in viable and increasing numbers again; complete clean-up of all toxic, nuclear and chemical waste sites by a specified date.

Just imagine – a possible brief historical overview, looking back from the year 2100

21st Century History of Ecological Restoration

1999 The 21st Century is declared the 'Century of Restoring the Earth' by the United Nations

2003 The Earth Restoration Service is launched, enrolling young volunteers from all over the world in essential restoration projects.

2015 Project Green Sahel is initiated, enlisting military personnel in restoration and tree planting work in the Sahel region.

2025 50 years after the end of the Vietnam War, the government announces that forest cover has been restored from 22% to 58% of the land.

2037 Chemical fertilisers are completely phased out and all the world's agriculture becomes organic, with immediate benefit to the health of people, the land and wildlife.

2043 Wolves are reintroduced to Japan and to the Caledonian Forest in Scotland.

2047 The world is declared free of land mines, after a concerted 50 years mine removal campaign.

2064 Tiger numbers reach 10,000 in the wild and it's removed from the Endangered Species list.

2085 In the restored Atlantic rainforest of Brazil not far from Rio, a previously unknown monkey species is discovered and it is taken as a sign that evolution on our planet is back on track again.

2100 9 year old David asks his great-grandfather Kevin Featherstone, then aged 105, how the Healing of the Earth took place. Kevin replies: "It all started with individuals here and there, deciding to make a difference with their lives. When they began to work with Nature, rather than against her, seeming miracles took place—the Earth really responded to our love and care."

····

Knowledge, Earth and Future

" Let us not go over the old ground, let us rather prepare, for what is to come...."

— *Marcus Tullius Cicero*

SEARCH FOR TRUE KNOWLEDGE

Nature is concerned with the production of elementary things. But man from these elementary things produces an infinite number of compounds; although he is unable to create any element except another life like himself—that is, in his children.

Old alchemists will be my witnesses, who have never either by chance or by experiment succeeded in creating the smallest element which can be created by nature; however, the creators of compounds deserve unmeasured praise for the usefulness of the things invented for the use of men, and would deserve it even more if they had not been the inventors of noxious things like poisons and other similar things which destroy life or mind; for which they are not exempt from blame. Moreover, by much study and experiment they are seeking to create not the meanest of Nature's products, but the most excellent, namely, gold, true son of the sun in as much as of all created thing it has most resemblance to the sun. No created thing is more enduring, which has power over all other created things, reducing them to ashes, glass, or smoke. And if gross avarice must drive you into such error, why do you not go to the mines where Nature produces such gold, and there become her disciple? She will in faith cure you of your folly, showing you that nothing which you use in your furnace will be among any of the things which she uses in order to produce this gold. Here there is no quicksilver, no sulfur of any kind, no fire nor other heat than that of Nature giving life to our world; and she will show you the veins of the gold spreading through the blue lapis lazuli, whose color is unaffected by the power of the fire.

And examine well this ramification of the gold and you will see that the extremities are continuously expanding in slow movement, transmuting into gold whatever they touch; and note that there-in is a living organism which it is not in your power to produce.

— Leonardo Da Vinci

Education

D. C. Pitt

I shall never believe that god plays dice with the world
— Albert Einstein

Futurology (defined as the science of predicting future trends) has had a mixed history in recent years. Some have dismissed futurology as science fiction. Elsewhere futurology, though having an important place in planning processes, has failed to anticipate significant trends. In this paper, we try to show what the role of futurology might be in a specific area: environmental education. Our objective is not only to point to different scenarios, but also to indicate what actions are called for.

In futurology as in history, the starting point is inevitably the present. The past and the future can only be viewed from changing contemporary concepts and situations. For this reason, it seems, every generation rewrites its history. But future directions need not, should not stem from all factors in the present situation. A major reason, in fact, why both futurology and education are becoming more important is the potential for anthropogenic change, the shift, to use Vernadsky's model of the world, from a biosphere to a noosphere, from parts which unconsciously interact to a system where conscious direction is more important.

Education may be said to be fundamental in any conscious direction because knowledge empowers the individual who possesses it. The alternative to education in political directions are those legal systems which tend to enforce norms of individual behaviour and which sooner or later lead to social, economic or political inequities.

Contemporary problems

Let us first try to set out the contemporary problems in environmental education and how these difficulties might best be resolved in the future. Some experts have argued, in fact that environmental education must develop in reaction to problems.

1. The big problems:

The big problems which influence the total situation and on which little impact has been made are—high levels of poverty in the Third World, species loss, habitat degeneration (especially desertification), pollution, armaments (especially nuclear) escalation. Despite some hopeful signs, most of the big problems remain big. Nor are these problems generally adequately dealt with in the various environment education curriculums, though there are some exceptions.

2. The declining influence of education:

Again, in the Third World particularly, an alarming number of children, even if appearing on formal rolls, are not, in fact, in school. The informal education sector, once hailed as near salvation, is too often in decline even in industrialized countries. Environmental education is bound to decline with the general education sector, even more so perhaps since there is seen to be a lesser relevance to vocational and technical goals. The consequence of all this is a spreading illiteracy.

3. The decline of traditional messages and influence of counterproductive ideas:

Of course, whatever happens to classes, inside or outside school, people are still exposed to incoming messages. Traditionally these messages were contained in informal socialization processes within the family, community etc. This traditional knowledge contained much useful environmental information, stressing often a harmony with nature and a sustainable development approach to conservation. This nexus is fast disappearing, particularly in the Third World, eroded particularly by massive migration to urban centres, but also by new competitive intrusive forces, of which the mass media are the most important.

4. Deficiencies in the delivery of environmental educational messages:

Some of the problems in the contemporary situation may be explained by deficiencies in those structures which generate environmental education. Important ideas like the World Conservation Strategy are too little known and there is too little participation in revisions. The belief seems to be gaining ground that action cannot wait for or does not require education and many actions go ahead without an educational component.

At the national level there may be too little cash as well, but also defects in communication, co-ordination with other partners, non-governmental as well as governmental, with scientists, with teachers, with students, in what should be an intersectoral, interdisciplinary, dialogical exercise. In Third World countries, particularly, there are too few materials, certainly those which reflect local or cultural contexts, or the latest thinking and debates.

5. Problems of democratisation and relevance of environmental education:

UNESCO and IBE have identified a number of key problems here–illiteracy (growing along with an expanding population and increases in juvenile work forces), neglected rural populations, slum dwellers, girls, minority groups, unequal opportunities, irrelevance to contemporary social and cultural situations and development needs, and inefficient educational systems. Each one of these has an environmental education dimension. Despite valiant efforts, many of these problems show little improvement in the developing world, and even in some industrialized countries where what has been called a fourth world—a subproletariat—is emerging.

Future Challenges

But for all the problems recognized, and sometimes overcome, for all the success stories, laudable though they may be, there remain very significant challenges for environmental education in the future which should be recognized. These can be summarized:

1. Environmental education does not and should not operate in a vacuum, but as part of a holistic system embracing the biosphere or noosphere systems. In the immediate context there are the changes in the education system itself, which affect and are affected by environmental education, though it has to be admitted that environmental education has been a follower rather than a leader. Two important, somewhat contradictory changes, can be pointed out. The first has been an expansion of education, formal and in some contexts informal, both quantitatively in terms of student numbers and qualitatively in the forms of media that are utilized. On the other hand, there has been a deschooling of education, though rarely in the forms that Ivan Illich sought. In addition, there is a philosophy in some Western countries to place an increased emphasis on vocational training, including notably job experience, and cut down expenditure on academic education. Finally, there is in industrialized countries a contraction due to demographic changes.

In this situation, there are clear challenges to environmental education. In the first place, efforts should be made to ensure that the maximum support is given to the expansion of education and that inroads, e.g. lowering of compulsory age, the reduction of time spent in education etc., are resisted. In a time when there are major technological advances, with enormous effects on the environment, education should expand. Otherwise there will not only be increasing problems of general illiteracy and innumeracy, but also the emergence of an inferior class who have not only very limited access to income, jobs or means of satisfying their own basic needs, but inadequate knowledge to resist adverse environmental changes.

The increasing vocational orientation of education may also present an opportunity since there are too rarely environmental education elements in apprenticeships or similar schemes. The demographic changes whereby the younger generation becomes proportionally smaller (a trend which is also occurring in developing countries and may increase if phenomena like the AIDS epidemic spread) mean a greater emphasis on adult education, public awareness etc.

2.   A second major challenge is to develop an appropriate response to the broader socio-economic changes. The World Conservation Strategy recognized the links between conservation and development. But some care should be taken to see that environmental education does not become a tool to facilitate a form of detrimental development which may occur sometimes, even when sustainability is emphasized. To some degree, the public thrust of environmental education might need to be sharpened. This means an increased emphasis on protected areas, on commons, on public utility and use in all environmental institutions, including notably small-scale involvement.

In capitalist countries there is a movement towards privatisation which may make environmental goals for the public good more difficult to achieve. Even if in general, the goals of environmental education should also be made to see that individuals, notably those influential in the multinational business sector, are aware of environmental ethics and constraints. To reach this power elite, special techniques are needed as well as other pressures, perhaps of the kind pioneered by Greenpeace and other NGOs.

The question of underlying ideological or ethical bases needs to be faced and thought through. In fact, conservation goals for the public good are found in a number of systems which may seem at first to be antithetical. There is common ground in orthodox socialist cosmologies, religious systems, feminist and youth ideologies, and indigenous people's movements, etc. The task for those who would prepare not only more effective but more equitable education materials needs to involve increasing dialogues among these groups and also to make strenuous efforts to provide the most authoritative scientific knowledge, framed in terms of the languages and subcultures from which many of the ideologies spring.

3. The role of science and scientists is in fact crucial in the process of a more successful environmental education. If Vernadsky is right in saying that we are in a new noospheric age, scientists have the major responsibility in providing not only an accurate assessment of environmental relationships, but in seeing that such knowledge is fully communicated to both governments and people. It is heartening to see that there is a quickening pace in scientific organizations both nationally and internationally at the highest level, as evidenced in such groups as the International Physicians Against Nuclear War and the Ecoforum for Peace, the latter group having given the highest priority to education.

4. But it is clear that, however appropriate the reaction is to new ideas, educational and scientific or socio-economic changes, there is a considerable need for clear, coordinated, rational plans and strategies at all levels down to the community. Although well served by a number of important strategies, the most significant in environmental education being that formulated at the intergovernmental meeting in Tbilisi in 1977, and also the World Conservation Strategy announced a year later in Ashakabad But still there is much to be done. Rereading Tbilisi, one is impressed by the comprehensiveness of the statement. But despite the important work following Tbilisi, carried out notably by the International Environment Education Program organized by UNESCO and UNEP, there remain important tasks, particularly in influencing the intractable big problems that we have talked about. It is sad to record that countries like the United States and Great Britain have chosen to withdraw from UNESCO, precisely at a time when a concerted effort could have produced major achievements.

The follow-up (or lack of it) to the World Conservation Strategy has been much more disappointing. Education was given prominence in the strategy. In 1986 there was an important review of the World Conservation Strategy in Ottawa, but that meeting did not produce clear recommendations and although the sponsors of the World Conservation Strategy have since decided to issue a revised version it is not clear what role environmental education will play in it.

What can be done about this situation? It is reasonably well understood what needs to be done at the pedagogical level. This has been clearly set out in the reports of the Tbilisi meeting as well as in more recent texts. The question of placing environmental education higher on the agenda of organizations like the IUCN is rather a question of politics and social dynamics, particularly within the international community in which the IUCN operates. Although WWF has given some priority to education, training and awareness, making this a campaign theme in 1986, its thrust is still in the funding world where public relations exercises rather than fundamental education or development tasks.

The IUCN's relationships with the UN system have not been strong enough either. UNEP, UNESCO, FAO and IUCN constitute a group, the ECG, which attempts to coordinate conservation activities, but much of environment education, especially the much needed action activities, seem to lie outside the purview of the Committee. Some clear association, or even incorporation of the IUCN into the international system, may be called for.

5. The final challenge, perhaps the greatest and certainly that with the most potential, is at the grassroots, community level. To be realistic, changes in the formal education system are going to be slow, at least as far as incorporating environmental education ideas. It is in the informal sector that the grassroots organizations can play a most significant role. In some countries, there is already a well-established infrastructure. One can note the millions of members of nature clubs in the Third World, possibly attached to schools. One should note, however, that there are many more informal movements which spring up at the grassroots, either unnoticed and unencouraged by outsiders or sometimes actively discouraged.

A good example is the now-famous Chipko movement in India, which means literally 'hug the trees'. Here originally groups of women physically stood between the trees of their village and the commercial loggers. Chipko is in fact a good example of the rather different emphasis given to environmental education in grassroots movements, and also in some avantgarde community participation projects. Knowledge remains important, indeed Chipko followers, like many indigenous groups, have a vast understanding of the intricacies of the ecosystems in which they live, but equally significant is the way in which knowledge is always wedded to and derived from action, where 'learning is doing'.

We may draw several conclusions from this brief survey:

— Environmental education should be the most significant priority in future conservation strategies and action plans.

— New emphasis are needed and particular attention should be paid to the informal education system, utilizing radio and open learning techniques in a lifelong context.

— Greater efforts should be made to coordinate international actions on environmental education with emphasis on encouraging dialogues between different cultural and social systems.

— Much more notice should be taken of what is happening at the grassroots, and ways sought of encouraging these populistic actions.

— Closer links should be developed in educational materials between ecological issues and the major contemporary global problems of armaments, poverty and injustice.

....   •

What should be done: An Agenda for Today

Peter H. Raven, Linda R. Berg, George B. Johnson.

He will manage the cure best who foresees what is to happen from the present condition of the patient.
— *Hippocrates*

The problems discussed in this book carry an urgent message to us all, that the explosive and unevenly distributed growth of an unprecedented human population is putting unsupportable strains on the global ecosystem. The long period of transition from a hunter-gatherer society, in which widely dispersed humans were one of millions of species of organisms, to a modern industrial society, in which humans consume, co-opt, or waste 40 percent of the total global productivity, has now reached a point where our traditional modes of operation seem increasingly unlikely to lead us to stability and prosperity. In the light of this grave threat to our common future, we must weigh our options carefully as we seek ways to avoid poisoning the air we breathe and the water we drink, to avoid exterminating the organisms that we will need to build a stable life for our children, and to collectively and sustainably use the biosphere. There are a number of critical areas where significant progress can be made as we approach the year 2000, and we shall now discuss some of the concerns that we consider to be top priorities for global attention.

1. Population stability must be attained throughout the world, and the industrialized countries must assist others in carrying out their plans in this respect. It is especially important for industrialized countries to attain stable population levels, since their people consume such a disproportionately large share of what the world is capable of producing. There is no hope for a peaceful world without overall population stability, and no hope for regional economic sustainability without regional population stability. International assistance for family planning should be increased, with the United States continuing to play a leading role in the overall effort, as urged by the participants in the Cairo Conference on Population and Development in 1994.

2. **Women's rights** need to find fuller expression everywhere. Ensuring that all women have access to the full range of human opportunities would address environmental problems in two significant ways. First, it would greatly accelerate our progress toward global population stability. Second, because we will need all of the talent available in order to build a sustainable society, we cannot afford to limit any individual's potential for contributing to this effort.

3. **New energy sources** must be sought. The greenhouse effect associated with increasing concentrations of carbon dioxide and other gases in the atmosphere ought to stimulate research into alternative energy sources. Even if we officially choose to believe that the supplies of fossil fuels such as coal and oil are infinite, burning them in the quantities we do now is certainly not an environmentally sound practice. To make major changes in our sources of energy will require so high a level of readjustment that the effort must be begun well before it is to have a significant impact. Renewable energy sources such as solar/hydrogen power and biomass production should be explored while there is still time to accomplish changes.

4. **A comprehensive energy plan** must be implemented for the world. At present, three fourths of the world's people who live in developing countries use about 20 percent of the world's industrial energy. Their numbers are growing rapidly, however, and even without any increase in their standard of living, these countries will use much larger quantities of energy in the future. If and when they industrialize, and if there has been a global

consensus on limiting carbon dioxide in the atmosphere, we who live in the industrial nations of the world will find ourselves insisting that developing countries not burn coal, or that they take steps to remove gases from coal smoke that are far more rigorous

---

Box 21.1. WOMEN & THE EARTH

We live in a savage industrial world dominated by technologies, markets and exploitation. Never before in history have poor women been subjugated and repressed so severely as they are today because of the social chauvinism of men, worsening economic inequities and outrageous rape of the earth.

The impact of the deterioration of the natural environment on women has been cruel and seldom recognized. In the societies of the developing world, women have become the ultimate beast of burden and they have remained silent sufferers. Add to that the heavy burden of the children they bear - on an average six in Africa and four in Asia-Pacific.

In India, for every two literate men, one woman is educated; in Bangladesh, for every ten educated persons, seven are men and three are women.

A society, which allows such disproportionately low opportunities to women for development and which disregards the intrinsic value of natural resources, not only destroys the fifty percent of its human wealth in women, but in the end, it drives itself to an ultimate doom.

In such an anguished world, the only alternative for poor women is to link themselves with those who care for their future; they must demand full opportunity to be educated; they must become prime crusaders for protecting the scarce natural resources and the fragile ecological system. They must dedicate their life for a sublime purpose of building an egalitarian and sustainable society. They must transform all the institutions of exploitation of humans and nature. They should challenge oppression and destruction. They must work towards building a society, which preserves family, lives simply, protects nature, shares resources and values equity. Their goal should be to create a society of love, joy and harmony.

Source : Extract from the "Women and the Earth", Dr. Rashmi Mayur

and expensive than any we have used in our own countries. Such a strategy will seem unlikely to prevail—unless we all share in paying for it. The key is for those of us who live in the industrialized nations to realize that the implementation of a comprehensive energy plan for the developing world is a necessary ingredient for our own future security as well as for global stability.

5. Regional co-operation will be necessary to solve many pollution and conservation problems. Acid precipitation, for example, is a problem that must be solved regionally. A country, such as the United Kingdom or the United States, that "exports" acid precipitation to other countries by erecting tall smokestacks with inadequate scrubbers to remove sulfates, saves money, but it causes other countries to incur substantial costs and may cause them to adopt highly negative and ultimately dangerous attitudes toward them.

6. Soil and water must be better conserved. Plans for the sustainable use of the soil and water of all regions of the world must be developed, with provisions for sustainable forms of agriculture and forestry. Underdeveloped countries can achieve stability only if their best lands—those capable of sustainable productivity—are developed properly and if appropriate land-use schemes are implemented. Many experts agree that all of the agricultural and forestry needs of the poor people who live in the tropics could certainly be met by proper development of lands that have already been deforested. It is a profound human tragedy that we are not accomplishing this development. Instead, the rural poor are ignored, left to "mine" undisturbed forests on a one-time basis, and so convert potentially renewable resources into non-renewable wasteland.

7. Biodiversity must be truly protected throughout the world. We live in a situation where up to one fourth, or more, of the world's species of plants, animals, fungi and micro-organisms are likely to become extinct over the next several decades. Once they are gone, they will be gone forever; their disappearance is the crime for which our descendants will be least likely to forgive us. Our entire sustainable use of the world's resources depends on the wise management of biodiversity, because we obtain individual products from individual kinds of organisms, and we depend on the management of communities of organisms, regardless of how poorly we understand them, for the global preservation of soil, water and air.

8. Biotechnology provides us with remarkable new opportunities for the improvement of agriculture and forestry systems, and should be utilized in the development of improved crops throughout the world. We simply cannot afford our current inefficient use of biological resources, or the hunger that results from insufficient supplies of food in many regions. A global effort should be made to utilize the tools that are available to us for the improvement of many traditional tropical crops, such as manioc and yams, and for the development of additional ones that can be grown in areas not now under cultivation.

9. Individual values could use improvement, particularly among those making economic decisions. Often, businesspeople acquire assets and manage them guided strictly by economic considerations, without thinking about the serious environmental consequences of their actions. Many of these consequences have been discussed in this book. New methods of conducting business that internalize environmental costs are emerging, as are new work patterns such as telecommuting, in which travel is minimized.

What kind of world do we want?

Perhaps the most important single lesson to have learned from this textbook is that those of us who live in industrialized countries are the core of the problem facing the global ecosystem today. We number less than one quarter of the world's people, and our activities alone are more than sufficient to create global instability. For example, United States, with 4.5 percent of the world's population, generates about 21 percent of the world's carbon dioxide. Similar relationships can be demonstrated in almost any area of resource consumption, indicating clearly that the industrialized countries of the world must act forcefully to reduce their levels of consumption if we are all going to be able to attain stability.

To put it concisely, we must radically change our view of the world and adopt new ways of thinking, or we will perish together. We must learn to understand, respect, and work with one another, regardless of the differences that exist between us. The most heartening aspect of the situation that we confront is that people, given the motivation, do have the ability to make substantial changes.

At the deepest level, the most critical environmental problems, from which all others arise, are our own attitudes and values. We are totally out of touch and out of balance with the world, and until we reconnect and readjust in some significant way, all solutions will be stopgap ones. As a society we don't feel part of the global ecosystem; we feel separate, above it, and therefore in a position to consume and abuse without thought of consequences. This book has been about consequences. In the last 30 yeas and especially in the last decade, we have come to recognize the nature of the impact of human activity on the biosphere. We now understand this impact enough to know that we cannot continue to act as we have been acting and expect any sort of viable future for our species. If all we do as a result of this new knowledge is to make some shifts in consumer choices and write a few letters, it won't be nearly enough.

Your generation must become the next pioneers. A pioneer is one who ventures into unexplored territory, a process that is simultaneously terrifying and profoundly exciting. The unexplored territory in this case is the development of a truly different way for humans to exist in the world. No models exist for this kind of change. You must forge a new revolution, akin in scope and effect to the Agricultural Revolution or the Industrial Revolution, yet totally different because it must be deliberate. You must help create the political will for it with your numbers and your commitment. You must create the economic power with your thoughtful decisions as both consumers and leaders. You must create social change with your acceptance and respect of the differences between peoples.

....

Cultural of Permanance

Christopher Flavin

The challenge of making a sustainable society is predicated on coming in accordance with natural law, the linear economic system of input and output consumes more than it needs and produces waste which depends on intergenerational caretaking. It is time to take only as needed, leave the rest and make plans for intergenerational peace with the earth.

— *Winona La Duke*

Humanity now faces a challenge that rivals any in our history: reaching a new balance with nature while continuing to expand economic opportunities for the billions of people who still lack a decent standard of living. And as we face this daunting task, hope may be the most valuable commodity of all.

To master our problems, it is not enough that we be aware of them. We need a realistic expectation of surmounting them, and a viable strategy for doing so. Going backward to achieve balance with the natural world is hardly an acceptable choice. But at the cusp of a new millennium, what does moving forward mean?

We can anticipate only the rough outlines of a sustainable society—a blueprint based on some fundamental principles. Just as any aircraft, from an ultralight to a jumbo jet, must abide by the laws of aerodynamics, so must a lasting society achieve ecological harmony. At some point both the oceans and the atmosphere must be stabilized, and human demands must reach a new accommodation with the other forms of life on earth.

Less–polluting, less resource-intensive technology is one key to a society that can stand the test of time. But good science and engineering alone will not suffice. New values could be just as crucial to our future prosperity, and perhaps to our very existence.

Meeting the energy and material needs of the next century may be one of the easier hurdles we face, since today's oil and coal fields could be replaced by fields of solar generators and wind turbines located in remote deserts and plains.

Even in the Information Age we still live in a material world, and restoring our balance with nature will mean finding new ways of providing the millions of tons of metals, wood, cement and plastics that we depend on. Today we clear vast forests and rip open the earth to obtain many of those materials. We leave behind denuded landscapes and toxic wastepiles.

A better way is to close the loop—recycling virtually all the materials we use and designing everything from newspapers to buildings so as to minimize their materials requirements. Recycling programs in European and North American cities have in the space of a decade reduced the amount of household waste more than 50%, and some cities are aiming for 90%.

Products such as computers and automobiles are being redesigned for easy reuse. Some leading companies, for example, are producing a new generation of cars that can be quickly dismantled, with most of the remnants suitable for use in new vehicles or other items. Virtually eliminating waste and greatly reducing our dependence on virgin materials once seemed like a pipe dream, but it has now become a practical goal.

We will have to curb production of plastics and other petroleum-based materials. One promising idea is a carbohydrate economy—replacing petrochemicals with biologically derived materials that could be used for everything from plastic kitchen wrap to automobile bodies. David Morris of the Institute for

Local Self-Reliance in the U.S. believes that a fraction of the millions of tons of cornstalks, rice straw and other agricultural waste produced each year could substitute for most plastics.

Among the most difficult jobs will be feeding more than 8 billion people in the water-short world of the next century. Biotechnology certainly has a role to play in raising grain yields and making crops less demanding of water and less vulnerable to pests. But a shift in diets may also be needed. More than a third of the world's grain goes to feed animals that in turn produce meat, eggs and dairy products. This gives humans a protein-and fat-rich diet, but the conversion process is inefficient. If the world's affluent were to consume less meat—living a little lower on the food chain—it would be easier to provide a healthy diet for all. The trick will be to develop tasty and healthy vegetable products, some of which may be nearly indistinguishable from meat.

Another essential element of a sustainable society is a better balance between cities and the countryside. New land-use policies are needed to slow the spread of urban areas, which pave over thousands of square kilometers of farmland and wild areas each year. Inevitably cities will be better off if they are less sprawling, with improved public transportation and convenient footpaths.

For a glimpse of the future, look at Curitiba, Brazil, where a compact urban design and one of the world's best bus systems allow easy travel without cars. And well-planned government programs have helped Curitiba reduce homelessness, infant mortality and violence to levels well below those in other Brazilian cities. The future also beckons in Copenhagen, where free public bicycles and 300 km of bikeways enable nonmotorists to get around.

Information technology can help people do their jobs while traveling less and using fewer materials. Entrepreneurs in developing countries are providing satellite television and cellular phone service to villages without stringing millions of kilometers of copper wires or cutting thousands of trees into poles. Teleconferencing enables businesses to bring employees on distant continents together without consuming a drop of jet fuel. In the future more and more people are likely to work at home, using a modem to communicate with bosses.

Industries, too, could be transformed. Most of them are based on the extraction, processing and manufacture of physical materials, which consume resources and fuels in the process. But some pioneering companies have developed factories that drastically reduce emissions by using the effluent from one industrial process as raw material for another. Kalunberg Denmark has established a network of a dozen symbiotic industries. Ash from a power-plant smokestack is used to manufacture cement, while the waste from trout farms and pharmaceutical plants is used to fertilize nearby fields. Researchers at the United Nations University in Tokyo have started a $12 million Zero emissions Research Initiative that aims one day to make producing pollution from a factory as unacceptable as dumping sewage in the backyard is today.

The biggest challenge of all, however, may be within ourselves. The dramatic economic advances of the past century have been driven in part by a culture of materialism, and accelerated growth seems to be a universally accepted goal. But as environmental activist Ed Abbey once said, "Growth for the sake of growth is the ideology of the cancer cell." Unending, indiscriminate material expansion will destroy the earth's biosphere just as malignancy lays waste to the human body.

In the future we will have to focus on the quality of growth, not the amount. More software, services or human ideas do not have the environmental impact that more roads, buildings and

Box 22.1. BUILDING ECO-VILLAGES

"An eco-village is a human scale, full-featured settlement which integrates human activities harmlessly into the natural environment, supports healthy development and can be continued into the indefinite future."

Robert Gilman in his report "Eco-Villages and Sustainable Communities" (1991) offers the above definition.

"Eco-villages are sustainable settlements in urban or rural settings respecting and restoring the circulatory systems of the four elements: earth, water, fire and air in nature and in people.

This definition was accepted when 15 projects in Denmark created a national organization of eco-villages in 1991.

Earth - the element representing physical structures

— Bio-regional, local, organic food production. Plant and animal systems respect this beautiful cycle. Taking matter from agribusiness into big cities and - when digested - disposing of it in the seas and dumps is not respecting the cycle. Bioregional, organic food production is an appropriate way of providing up to 80% of local food supply, thus ensuring the local circulation of matter.

— When we build our settlements we use local, natural, non-toxic building materials as far as possible. Clay, wood, stone, grass, gravel and straw. The question to ask is: Can they be recycled?

— Part of the building process will be the integration of renewable energy systems, waste water treatment and food supply. All planners should learn to think holistically.

— Lifecycle analysis is a must. Industry leaders must ask themselves when using materials for producing goods: Are the products necessary and useful? Can we use local, natural, non-toxic materials? Can the product be produced in a way so that the matter can be recycled? Earth restoration is part of most eco-villages. The humus layer has in most places been drastically reduced. We must rebuild it through earth care and composting. Tree planting is a necessity in most of areas of the planet.

Water - the element representing infrastructure.

— Biological wastewater treatment, watersheds, care of surface water and protection of the quality and level of the ground water are intrinsic to eco-villages.

— Integrated, renewable energy systems. According to the Brundtland Commission of September 1987, we should reduce our use of energy by 90% in the North. (In the South they need an increase of 50%). The energy created by the sun, wind, water and biomass is at our disposal in sufficient amounts if and when we decide to use them responsibly. Renewable, integrated energy systems are being developed by many grassroots initiatives. Villages in the south may yet avoid the worst excesses of the North.

— The eco-village is a lifestyle which limits transportation of foods and goods, commuting, transportation for "escapes into nature", tourism etc. It will take some time to transform our need for transportation and diminish the pressure on nature, which can be measured in carbon dioxide emissions. Alternative ways of transportation will have to be developed with emphasis on collective transport.

— Communication can in some cases be an alternative to physical transportation, for example exchange of information electronically: telephone, telefax, e-mail and internet. Every village will however need only one information centre initially—and it can be done with known technology.

Fire—the element that represents social structure

— Community level decision-making. At the Find horn eco-village conference in October 1995, the general feeling was that the optimal size for a community was about 500 persons. People from all over the world agreed on this. Some suggested as high as 2-3000 persons, but no one felt that larger entities were desirable. We need decision structures which are truly democratic.

People want community back. They want to reclaim the right to resolve their own conflicts, make their own rules, to take care of their children, the old and weak, take care of their own health and live full lives. Much of this will have to be relearned. Conflict resolution in communities will be a big issue everywhere. And it takes a village to educate a child.

— The economic system will in the long run have to be modified to suit and support local communities. This includes "foreign aid" and the World Bank programs for the South. Economics is, after all, a human invention.

It can be reinvented to serve rather than to rule. Local economics have to be stimulated so that money can circulate locally without dissipating into the big cities. LETS (local exchange trade systems) are being set up in many places.

— The subject of preventive and general health care is one area that must be transformed. We may save up to 80% of health costs in the North once we create healthy lifestyles and take back the responsibility for our health.

Air—the element that represents culture

— Creativity and expression of the uniqueness of every human being through personal development (unfoldment) is part of individualism within the community as opposed to conformity in mass society.

— People create festivals, rituals and celebrations as ways of manifesting their interconnectedness to fellow beings and nature. The feeling of connectedness binds us together and gives us a feeling of joy and belonging.   ,

— A New Holographic, Circulatory World View is required. Global consciousness could be the name for this new paradigm. What happens to nature happens to our bodies. That is the holographic principle. It is manifested in the ancient wisdom cultures of the world as also now Western science is realising. Let us cherish the old cultures and the world's spiritual leaders. And let us fully understand the teachings of modern science.

— There are many paths towards integrating this new global consciousness in our thinking and behaviour. It takes time and effort to eradicate the errors of Western industrial culture in our bodies and thinking. The main thing is to start this journey and accept the necessity of it. Eco-villages are perfect places for this process to develop.

How to create an eco-village?

The process will be different, depending on where you start, but the vision seems to be common to people all over the planet. Do you start in the North or in the South? In the country or the city? In an existing settlement or on virgin land? Is your motivation mainly ecological, social or spiritual? Why is it so difficult? Why are there so few eco-villages? Creating an eco-village is defining a whole new culture. Getting a piece of land, getting a motivated group together, getting the vision down into a concrete design. Designing houses, an integrated energy system, food production system, storing of food and an economic system, is necessary. All areas of life have to be redefined. At the same time as you do all this you may have to earn money and bring up a family. And fight authorities and administration to get permissions. This is an almost impossible task. And yet people are out there doing it—without any support.

Source : "The Earth is Our Habitat", by Gaia Trust and The Global Eco-Village Network, What is an ecovillage, Hilclur Jackson, June 1996. For more information visit :- http://www.gaia.org

autos do. The goal is to keep economic opportunities and jobs growing—particularly in the developing world—but to minimize the materials, energy and pollution accompanying the growth.

The new era calls for what environmental writer Alan Durning describes as a "culture of permanence"—meeting the needs of the current generation without jeopardizing the prospects of the next. Above all, survival will require a renewed appreciation for nature. Our ancestors could see their dependence on the natural world daily. They viewed trees and animals as sacred and treated them with respect. Today we need a return of that reverence. As Harvard biologist Stephen Jay Gould puts it, "We cannot win this battle to save species and environments without forging an emotional bond between ourselves and nature." Unless we follow Gould's advice, we may not be able to save ourselves either.

••••

Party's End

What can I say without touching my palms to the land?
To whom shall I turn without rain?
I have never set foot in the countries I lived in,
every port was a port of return:
I have no post cards, no keepsakes of hair
from important cathedrals: I have built what I could
out of natural stone, like a native, open-handed,
I have worked with my reason, unreason, my caprices,
my fury, and poise: hour after hour
I have touched the domains of the lion
and the turbulent tower of the bee:
having seen what there was to be seen,
having handled the clay and the loam, the spray and the rock,
with those who remember my footprints and words,
the tendrils of plants whose kisses remain on my mouth,
I say: "Here is my place," stripping myself down in the light
and dropping my hands in the sea,
until all is transparent again
there under the earth, and my sleep can be tranquil.

— Pablo Neruda

243

Copyright Acknowledgments

- Bertrand Russell: 'The Free Man's Worship' from *Why I am not a Christian*, edited by Paul Edwards; Touchstons book, Simon and Schuster, Inc., Rockefeller Centre, 1230 Avenue of the Americans, New York, NY 10020, 1957.

- Herbert Marwse: 'Ecology and Revolution' from *Ecology: Key concepts in critical theory*, edited by Carolyn Merchant; Humanities press International Inc., 165 First Avenue, Atlantic Highlands, New Jersey, 07716-1289, 1994.

- Carloyn Merchant: 'Green politics' from *Radical Ecology: the search for a livable world;* Routledge, Chapman and Hall, Inc., 29 West 35 Street, New York, NY 10001, 1992.

- Seattle, Indian Chief: Mother Earth from *A Diet for a New America* by John Robbins; Stillpoint publishing division of Stillpoint International, Inc., Box 640, Meetinghouse road, Walpole, NH0360, 1987.

- Christina Salat: 'Indigenous people recruit for the new frontier' from *The Humanist: the magazine of critical inquiry and social concern;* 7 Harwood drive, P. O. Box, 1188, Amherst, NY 14226-7188, Nov-Dec, 1998.

- Holmes Rolston, III: 'Natural Value: A theory of environmental ethics' from *Environmental Ethics: duties to and values in the natural world;* Temple University Press, Philadelphia 19122, 1988.

- Severen Cullis Suzuki; 'An appeal for future generations' from *Earth Island Journal;* Earth Island Institute, 300 Broadway, Suite 28, San Francisco, California, 94133, Summer 1994.

- Lamont C. Hempel: 'Earthkeeping: the politics of a Sustainable Future' from *Environmental Governance: the global challenge;* Island Press, 1781 Connecticut Avenue, NW, Suite 300, Washington, D. C., 20009, 1996.

- Allan Teathestpme; 'Proposal for the U. N. To declare 21st century as the century for restoring the Earth' from *Draft Proposal* by A. Teathestone presented to GAIA Trust International Network Seminar, September, 1998.

- Leonardo Da Vinci: 'Search for true knowledge' from *The notebooks of Leonardo Da Vinci* by Irma A. Richter Oxford University Press, 1952.

- David C. Pitt: 'Education' from *The Future of the Environment: the social dimensions of conservation and ecological alteration,* edited by David C. Pitt; Routledge, 11 New Fetter lane, London, EC4P4EE, 1988.

- Peter H. Raven, Linda R. Berg and George B. Johnson: 'What should be done: An agenda for today' from *Environment: 1995 version;* Saunders college publishing, Harcourt Brace and Company, 6277 SeaHarbour drive, Orlando, Klonda, 32887-6777, 1995.

- Christopher Flavin: 'Culture of permanence' from *Time: Special Issue,* Time, Inc., Rockefeller Center, New York, NY 10020-1993.

246

Bibliography

- Allen Robert; *'HOW TO SAVE THE WORLD: Strategy for World Conservation'*, prepared by the International Union for Conservation of Nature & Natural resources (IUCN) based on world conservation strategy, with advice and assistance and financial co-operation from UNEP & WWF, Kugan Page Ltd., London, 1980.

Krishnamurti J; *'EDUCATION AND THE SIGNIFICANCE OF LIFE'*, Kirshnamurti Writing Inc., 1953. Victor Gonnancz Ltd., London, 1978.

Disch, Robert; *'THE ECOLOGICAL CONSCIENCE: Values for Survival'*, Prentice Hall Inc., New Jersey, 1970.

Manchu, Rigoberta; 'I, RIGOBERTA MANCHU: An Indian in Guatemala', Verso and NLB, 1984.

Gareett, Roger .M, ed; *'EDUCATION AND DEVELOPMENT'*, St. Martin's Press, New York, 1984.

Bhatia, S. C.; *'ENVIRONMENTAL CONSCIOUSNESS AND ADULT EDUCATION'*, Environment Division, Department of Science, Govt. of India, New Delhi, 1980.

Gore, Al; *'THE EARTH IN BALANCE: forging a new common purpose'*, Earthscan Publications Ltd., Houghton Mifflin Company, Published in India by Viva Books Pvt. Ltd., New Delhi, 1992.

Periera, Winnin & Seabrook, Jeremy; *'ASKING THE EARTH: The Spread of unsustainable Development'*, The Other India Goa Press, Mapusa, India, 1990.

Bowler, Peter J; *'THE NORTON HISTORY OF ENVIRONMENTAL SCIENCES'*, W. W. Norton & Company, Inc., New York, 1992.

Pitt, Davit C., ed; *'THE FUTURE OF THE ENVIRONMENT': The social dimensions of conservation & ecological alternatives'*, Routledge, London, 1988.

Dashefsky, Steven H.; *'ENVIRONMENTAL LITERACY'*, Randon House, Inc., New York/Canada, 1993.

Davis, John, ed; *'THE EARTH FIRST! READER'*, International Institute for Sustainable Future, Mumbai, India, 1995.

Robinson, Andrew; *'EARTH SHOCK: CLIMATE, COMPLEXITY & THE FORCES OF NATURE'*, Thames & Hudson Ltd., London 1993.

- Ward, Barbara & Dubos, Rene; *'ONLY ONE EARTH: The care & maintainance of a small planet'*, Andre Deutsh Ltd., 1972.

- Kulik J. A & Kulik C. L; *'EFFECTIVENESS OF COMPUTER BASED INSTRUCTION: An updated analysis'*, Ann Arbour, Centre for research on learning and teaching, University of Michigan, 1991.

- Dobson A; *'GREEN POLITICAL THOUGHT'*, Harper Collins, London, 1990.

- Taylor L. & Jenkins P; *'TIME TO LISTEN: The human aspect in development'*, Intermediate Technology Publication, Rugby, 1989.

- Grieg S, Pike G & Selby. D, eds; *'EARTHRIGHTS: Education as if the planet really mattered'*, World Wildlife Fund/Kogan Page, London,1987.

- Lovelock J. E; *'GAIA: A new look of life on Earth'*

- Brown L. K.; *'STATE OF THE WORLD 1989. WORLD WATCH INSTITUTE: Report on Program Toward a Sustainable Society, 1989.*

- DiChiro G.; *'ENVIRONMENTAL EDUCATION: Practise and Possibility'*, 1987.

- Blight S, Sautter R, Silbey J & Smith. R (eds); *'OUR COMMON FUTURE – Pathways for Environmental Education,* 1990.

- Champain P & Inman S; *'THINKING FUTURES: Making space for environmental education in ITE – a hand book for educators*, 1996

- Mauri Ahlberg (Editor), Walter L. Filho (Editor) / Paperback Date Published: August 1998, *'ENVIRONMENTAL EDUCATION FOR SUSTAINABILITY: Good Environment, Good Life'*.

- Abrams R. (Editor) / Paperback Date Published: October 1997, *'ENVIRONMENTAL EDUCATION FOR THE NEXT GENERATION, 1996: Professional Development and Teacher Training'*

- Walter Leal Filho (Editor), Farruk Tahir (Editor) / Paperback / Published 1998, *'DISTANCE EDUCATION AND ENVIRONMENTAL EDUCATION ' (Environmental Education, Communication and Sustainability, Vol.2).*

- Baird Callicott J. (Editor), et al / Paperback / Published 1996, *'EARTH SUMMIT ETHICS: Toward a Reconstructive Postmodern Philosophy of Envrionmental Education' (Suny Series in Constructive Postmodern Thought).*

- Steve Van Matre / Paperback / Published, 1988, *'EARTHKEEPERS:Four Keys for Helping Young People Live in Harmony With the Earth'*

- Bowers C. A. / Paperback / Published, 1995, *'EDUCATING FOR AN ECOLOGICALLY SUSTAINABLE CULTURE: Rethinking Moral Education, Creativity, Intelligence, and Other Modern Orthodoxies (Suny Series I).'*

- Bowers C. A. / Paperback / Published, 1993, *'EDUCATION, CULTURAL MYTHS AND THE ECOLOGICAL CRISIS: Toward Deep Changes (Suny Series in the Philosophy of Education)'.*

- Mark K., M. S. Mitchell, et al., / Paperback / Published 1996, *'FIELD MANUAL FOR WATER QUALITY MONITORING: An Environmental Education Program for Schools.'*

- Jonathan Collett (Editor), et al., / Paperback / Published 1996, *'GREENING THE COLLEGE CURRICULUM: A guide to Environmental Teaching in the Liberal Arts'.*

- Maury M. Breecher, Shirley Linde (Contributor) / Ppaerback / Published 1992, *'HEALTHY HOMES IN A TOXIC WORLD: Preventing, Identifying and Eliminating Hidden Health Hazards in Your Home'*

- Lenore Hendler Miller / Paperback / Published 1986, *'THE NATURE SPECIALIST: A Complete Guide to Program and Activities.'*

- Martin Teitel, Jeremy Rifkin / Paperback / Published 1992, *'RAIN FOREST IN YOUR KITCHEN: The Hidden Connection Between Extinction and Your Supermarket.'*

- John Harte, et al., / Hardcover / Published 1991, *'TOXICS A TO Z: A Gunde to Everyday Pollution Hazards.'*

- Terrific Science Press / Paperback / Published 1998, *'UNDERSTANDING GARBAGE AND OUR ENVIRONMENT '.*

Glossary

acid mine drainage Precipitation that is acidic as a result of both sulfur and nitrogen oxides forming acids when they react with water in the Earth's atmosphere; partially due to the combustion of coal; includes acid rain, acid snow, and acid fog.

acrylonitrile Used in making paints, dyes, plastics, synthetic fibers and pesticides. Causes cancer and nerve damage. Causes headaches, weakness and skin irritation. Inhaled or absorbed through skin.

alternative agriculture Agricultural methods that rely on beneficial biological processes and environmentally friendly chemicals rather than conventional agricultural techniques. Also called *sustainable* or *low-input agriculture*.

artificial eutrophication Overnourishment of an aquatic ecosystem by nutrients such as nitrates and phosphates. In artificial eutrophication the pace of eutrophication is accelerated quite rapidly due to human activities such as agriculture and discharge from sewage treatment plants.

benzene Found in motor fuels, solvents, inks, paints, plastics and rubber. Used in making detergents, explosives, drugs and dyes. Causes cancer and damages nervous system and brain. Inhaled and absorbed through skin and eyes.

biological control A method of pest control that involves the use of naturally occurring disease organisms, parasites, or predators to control pests. Also called *biological pest control.*

biomass (1) A quantitative estimate of the total mass, expressed as the dry weight of all the organic material that comprises living organisms in a particular ecosystem. (2) Plant and animal materials used as fual.

bituminous coal The most common form of coal; produces a high amount of heat and is used extensively by electric power plants. Also called *soft coal.*

cadmium heavy, toxic metal used in metal coatings, solder, nickel plating, jewelry and catalytic converters in vehicles. Used in fertilizers. Crops grown in these fertilizers, such as tobacco, are high in cadmium. Smokers have high levels of cadmium. Attacks liver, lungs, kidney and blood. Causes cancer.

carbaryl   Made from di-isocyanate, the chemical that maimed and killed tens of thousands of people in Bhopal, India, In 1989, carbaryl causes birth defects in dogs and nervous system damage in people.

carcinogen Any substance that causes cancer or accelerates its development.

chlordane   Oil-based pesticide used in United States to kill termites. National Academy of Sciences finds no safe level. Banned in United States in 1980s. Most Americans have accumulated some in their bodies.

chlorinated hydrocarbon   A synthetic organic compound that contains chlorine and is used as a pesticide (for example, DDT) or an industrial compound (for example, PCBs).

clearcutting   A forest management technique that involves the removal of all trees from an area at a single time.

compost   A natural soil and humus mixture that improves soil fertility and soil structure.

conservation tillage   A method of cultivation in which residues from previous crops are left in the soil, partially covering it and helping to hold it in place until the newly planted seeds are established.

DDT Dichlorodiphenyltrichloroethane. Pesticide used throughout world to kill insects. Used on food, as mosquito fogger, and in homes until 1972 when banned in the United States. Causes cancer. Accumulates in human tissue. Americans show DDT in bodies twenty yeas after ban. Still used in other countries. Can contaminate imported foods.

decibel (dB)   A numerical scale that expresses the relative loudness of sound.

deep ecology   The conviction that all creatures have the right to exist and that humans should not cause the extinction of other living things.

dieldrin   Organochlorine pesticide used on crops. Very persistent in environment, accumulates in human fat. Causes cancer and is toxic to nervous system. Absorbed through skin and lungs, also ingested.

dioxin   Highly toxic chemical formed in production of weed killers, incineration of wastes, or when chlorine contacts wood material and heat. Causes cancer and birth defects. Called the most toxic chemical ever made. Builds up in virtually all animal and human tissues. Found in milk cartons, disposable diapers, napkins, coffee filters and bleached white paper.

dust dome A dome of heated air that surrounds an urban area and contains a lot of air pollution. See *urban heat island.*

entropy   A measure of the randomness or disorder of a system.

ethylbenzene   Contained in gasoline, pesticides, paints and used in making styrene and synthetic rubber. Primary human exposure from vehicle exhaust (smog) and handling gasoline products. Causes diseases of liver, lungs, kidneys, skin and lungs. Symptoms include headaches and dizziness. Absorbed through eyes, skin and lungs.

eutrophication   The enrichment of a lake or pond by nutrients. Eutrophication that occurs naturally is a very slow process in which the lake gradually fills in and converts to a marsh, eventually disappearing.

genetic resistance   An inherited characteristic that decreases the effect of a pesticide on a pest. Over time, the repeated exposure of a pest population to a pesticide causes an increase in the number of individuals that can tolerate the pesticide.

global commons   Those resources of our environment that are available to everyone but for which no single individual has responsibility.

immunotoxic   Term describing toxic chemicals that reduce the body's own defenses against disease.

indoor pollution   A condition in any building where chemicals from glues, carpets, pesticides, wall coverings, paints, office machinery, tobacco smoke, etc., reach unhealthy levels. The condition is added to by other pollutants such as dust, molds, carbon monoxide and dioxide. It occurs most often when the building lacks adequate ventilation and fresh air.

lead   Heavy metal used in batteries, pipes, solder, paints and gasoline manufacture. Primary human exposures: drinking water leached from plumbing; air from vehicle exhausts, smog and dust from lead-based paints. Accumulates in body and damages brain and nervous system. Causes lowered IQ, stomach disorders, fatigue and behavioral problems

marasmus   A condition of progressive emaciation that is especially common in children and is caused by a diet low in both total calories and protein.

methyl bromide   Colorless gas or liquid used to treat homes for termites. Residues in carpets, drapes and leather furniture make people ill. Suspected of causing cancer. Toxic to lungs, skin and brain.

monosodium glutamate   Synthetically produced taste enhancer added to food. Products high levels of glutamate in body; linked to nervous system and brain disorders. An excitotoxin. Contained in food additives not listing it specifically as ingredient.

mulch   Material placed on the surface of soil around the bases of plants. A mulch helps to maintain soil moisture and reduce soil erosion. Organic mulches have the additional advantage of decomposing over time, thereby enriching the soil.

neo-Malthusians   Economists who hold that developmental efforts are hampered by a rapidly expanding population.

nondegradable   A chemical pollutant (such as the toxic elements mercury and lead) that cannot be decomposed (broken down) by living organisms or other natural processes.

nuclear autumn   A moderate cooling of the global climate caused by dust and smoke hurled into the stratosphere after a nuclear after a nuclear war. The envisioned effects of a nuclear autumn are less severe than those of a nuclear winter. Compare *nuclear winter.*

nuclear winter   A catastrophic cooling of the global climate caused by dust and smoke hurled into the stratosphere after a nuclear war.

oligotrophic lake   A deep, clear lake that has minimal nutrients. Water in an oligotrophic lake contains a high level of dissolved oxygen.

ozone   A blue gas, O_3, that has a distinctive odor. Ozone is a human-made pollutant in one part of the atmosphere (the troposphere) but a natural and essential component in another (the stratosphere).

parts per million   The number of parts of a particular substance found in one million parts of air, water, or some other material. Abbreviated ppm. (parts per billion: ppb)

PCBs   Polychlorinated biphenyls. Invented in the 1930s and added to oil inside electrical devices to protect oil breakdown at high temperatures. They conduct electricity and resist heat, requiring three thousand degrees to bread down. Most PCBs made are still in the environment, despite being banned in the 1970s as toxic and cancer causing. Found in water, soil, fish, crops, animals and humans today.

photochemical smog A brownish-orange haze formed by complex chemical reactions involving sunlight, nitrogen oxides, and hydrocarbons. Some of the pollutants in photochemical smog include peroxyacyl nitrates (PANs), ozone and aldehydes.

photodegradable Breaking down upon exposure to sunlight.

photovoltaic (PV) solar cell   A wafer or thin-film device that generates electricity when solar energy is absorbed.

polyethylene   Plastic used in carpet, chewing gum, coffee stirrers, drinking glasses, food containers, plastic bags, garbage cans, toys and squeeze bottles. Suspected of causing cancer.

polyvinyl chloride   Plastic used in artificial grass, baby pants, cosmetics, crib bumpers, floor tiles, pipes, garden hoses, inflatable toys, pacifiers and shower curtains. Releases vinyl chloride that causes cancer and birth defects.

pyramid of biomass   An ecological pyramid that illustrates the total biomass (for example, the total dry weight of all living organisms in a community) at each successive trophic level.

pyramid of energy   An ecological pyramid that shows the energy flow through each trophic level of an ecosystem.

radon   A colorless, tasteless, radioactive gas produced during the radioactive decay of uranium in the Earth's crust.

saltwater intrusion   The movement of seawater into a freshwater aquifer located near the coast; caused by groundwater depletion.

selective cutting   A forest management technique in which mature trees are cut individually or in small clusters while the rest of the forest remains intact so that the forest can regenerate quickly (and naturally).

slash-and-burn agriculture   A type of shifting agriculture in which the forest is cut down, allowed to dry, and burned; the crops that are planted immediately afterwards thrive because the ashes provide nutrients. In a few years, however, the soil is depleted and the land must be abandoned.

solar pond   A technique to harvest the sun's energy by using a pond of water to collect solar energy.

solar thermal electric generation   A means of producing electricity in which the sun's energy is directed by mirrors onto a fluid-filled pipe; the heated fluid is used to generate electricity.

sterile male technique   A method of insect control that involves rearing, sterilizing, and releasing large numbers of males of the pest species.

synergy and synergism   The often unpredictable interactions of chemical substances, such as contaminants or drugs, that, when combined, enhance each other's effectiveness.

threatened species   A species in which the population is low enough for it to be at risk of becoming extinct, but not low enough that it is in imminent danger of extinction.

urban heat island Local heat buildup in an area of high population density. See *dust dome.*

water table The uppermost level of an unconfined aquifer, below which the ground is saturated with water.

western diseases A group of noninfectious diseases that are generally more commonplace in industrialized countries. Include obesity and heart disease.

xenoestrogen As their name implies, xenoestrogens are not natural estrogens. They are produced outside of the human body, but scientists have discovered that once they find their way into the human body a number of these structurally disparate petrochemicals, including a wide range of pesticides and industrial pollutants, have the uncanny ability to mimic estrogen, the primary feminizing hormone; they evoke "responses in the uterus (or other female reproductive organs) similar to those observed after administration of classical estrogens, such as estradiol".

zero population growth When the birth rate equals the death rate. A population with zero population growth remains the same size.

Wilderness State of nature in its original primal condition — without human. intervention."